EPIC

STORIES FROM THE GOSPELS

60 SESSIONS IN THE LIFE OF **JESUS**

FOR CELL GROUPS

**DARYL SMITH and BRIAN BABCOCK
with LYMAN COLEMAN**

Epic Stories from the Gospels:
60 Sessions in the Life of Jesus for Cell Groups
© 2020 by Daryl L. Smith and Brian D. Babcock, with Lyman Coleman.

Further resources and coaching: Check out **5QCentral.com**; or contact Daryl Smith at **DarylSmith432@gmail.com**.

Design by Carolyn B. Smith. Some photos purchased from Getty Images.

Some questions in this book are adapted from the *Serendipity Group Bible for Leaders: New Testament* (never-sold special edition); ©1999, Serendipity House. Used by permission of Lyman Coleman, editor.

ISBN: 9798664458480

DEDICATION

To Lyman and Margaret Osborne Coleman

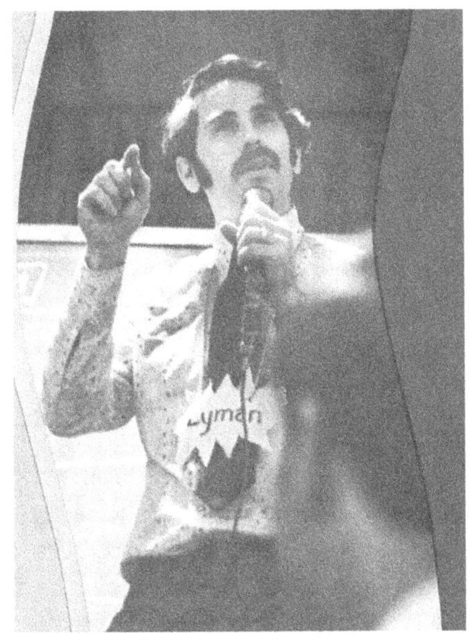

Lyman—
... A genius in group
formation principles
for more than 60 years,
... The founder of
Serendipity House,
... An amazing group resource
author—who is still writing,
... The creator of "frog-kissing"
workshops—equipper of thousands,
... A Spirit-empowered mentor
who taught us all
(whether we know him or not)
the transformational way of
Jesus that comes alive in biblical,
cell-group communities,
... Most of all, a special friend!

Margaret—
... "A 90-pound, fiery, wiry, passionate Celt from Great Britain,"*
... Lyman's lover, soulmate, muse,
... The one who "turned [Lyman's]
insecurity into serendipity—
'one surprise after another,'"*
... the gift-from-God partner.

*Those of us who've spent our lives
in growing cell group communities
owe both—Lyman and Margaret—a
lifetime of gratitude for the ministry
legacy they've given us; and thanks
to the God who gifted them to us!*

*From *A Love Story* by Lyman Coleman

*Serendipity has always been
known for "frog-kissing"—
releasing people to become the
best of what is inside them—in a
community of others who can see in
us things we don't see in ourselves.*

AUTHORS

Brian D. Babcock has served the Church for more than 45 years. He pastored in Texas and Kentucky, taught New Testament and spiritual formation at the undergraduate and graduate levels, facilitated the creation of two certificate-granting institutes to prepare ordained and lay leaders, hosted workshops for Christian education volunteers and small group leaders, and conducted biblical-studies and leadership workshops for local congregations.

In 2008 Brian founded a network to facilitate Christian ministries in inner-city settings. He and his wife, Carol, lead Faith and Finances workshops and English communication skills workshops for immigrant families.

Lyman Coleman is the 20th-century's premiere innovator in small group work. He first experienced "the power of the group" in a high-school Young Life chapter, and later applied those experiences to the coffee-house movement in the early- to mid-60s while at Baylor University and Biblical Seminary of New York. He then helped incorporate small-group dynamics into the Faith-at-Work movement led by Lloyd Ogilvie, Bruce Larsen and Keith Miller.

By 1970, Lyman was writing "Serendipity" training books for Word Publishing. That led to his "Serendipity House"—the source of hundreds of small-group resources and training for more than 500,000 small group leaders and participants.

Around 1980 Lyman began to develop study-Bible projects printed by Zondervan and, later, LifeWay. When Lyman's life was rocked by the death of his son, Kevin, and later his wife, Margaret, he found support in men's groups.

Whatever the specific project, Lyman has always helped people get past the superficial, to honestly struggle with how the Bible speaks to the lives of real people.

Daryl L. Smith is a leader-coach with 5Q/100 Movements (a missional coaching ministry), a cell-group leader trainer, and an emeritus professor of mentoring and leadership.

He has served in ministry roles for 40+ years—from leadership in local congregations to work as a teaching partner for Serendipity House.

Since Lyman Coleman first introduced him to small groups as a college freshman, each season of Daryl's life has circled around living in cell groups.

THANK-YOUS

Thanks to all the individuals and families who responded to the
Gather questions and allowed their pictures to be used in these pages:

Emily & Jesse Bachman family
Erik Bendoyro
Bruce & Marcy Brown
Steve & Jeannie Harper
Kailey Newkirk & family
Jason & Brooke Leadingham family
Meghan, Hannah & Sara Head & friends
Dawn & Blair Salmons family
Andrew & Emily Smith family
Jared & Niran Townsend
Our Thursday Night Group (brought together by COVID-19)

"Serendipity—The facility of making happy, chance discoveries" (Horace Walpole, 1743).

The Serendipity logo and frog used by permission of creator Lyman Coleman.

Serendipity: Facilitating happy, chance discoveries since 1965.

CONTENTS

START HERE 11

GROUP LEADER BASICS..14

THE EPIC STORIES

1. The Birth of Jesus Foretold—(Luke 1:26–38) 18
2. Mary Visits Elizabeth—(Luke 1:39–56) 21
3. An Angel Appears to Joseph—(Matthew 1:18–25) 24
4. The Birth of Jesus—(Luke 2:1–20)..27
5. Jesus Presented at the Temple—(Luke 2:21–40) 30
6. Young Jesus at the Temple—(Luke 2:41–52) 33
7. The Baptism & Temptation of Jesus—(Matthew 3:13–4:11)........36
8. Water to Wine—(John 2:1–12)..39
9. Jesus Teaches Nicodemus—(John 3:1–21) 42
10. Jesus & the Samaritan Woman—(John 4:7–30) 45

11. Jesus Rejected in Nazareth—(Luke 4:14–30) 48
12. The Calling of the Disciples—(Luke 5:1–11) 51
13. Jesus Heals a Paralytic—(Mark 2:1–12)..53
14. The Calling of Levi | New Wineskins—(Luke 5:27–39) 56
15. Jesus Calms the Storm—(Mark 4:35–41) 59
16. Jesus Heals a Bleeding Woman—(Mark 5:24–34) 61
17. Jesus Feeds 5,000—(Mark 6:30–44) 64
18. Jesus Walks on Water—(Matthew 14:22–33) 67
19. Healing a Demon-Possessed Man—(Luke 8:26–39).....................70
20. Ten Healed of Leprosy—(Luke 17:11–19) 73

21. Jesus Heals at the Pool—(John 5:1–15)..75
22. Jesus Heals a Man Born Blind—(John 9:1–34) 77
23. The Beatitudes—(Matthew 5:1–12)..80
24. Jesus Teaches Us to Pray—(Matthew 6:5–15)..............................83
25. Wise & Foolish Builders—(Matthew 7:24–29)................................85
26. Losing & Saving Life—(Matthew 16:13–28)....................................87
27. A Mother's Request—(Matthew 20:20–28) 90
28. Sheep & Goats—(Matthew 25:31–46) 93
29. Lord of the Sabbath—(Mark 3:1–6)..96
30. John Beheaded—(Mark 6:14–29) 99

31. The Transfiguration—(Mark 9:2–13) 102
32. The Rich Young Man—(Mark 10:17–31) 105
33. A Widow's Offering—(Mark 12:41–44) 108
34. Mary & Martha—(Luke 10:38–42) 110
35. Jesus Anointed at Bethany—(Mark 14:1–9) 112
36. Money & Possessions—(Luke 12:22–34) 115
37. Jesus Raises Lazarus—(John 11:17–44) 117
38. Zacchaeus—(Luke 19:1–10) 120
39. The Woman Caught in Adultery—(John 8:1–11) 123
40. Workers in the Vineyard—(Matthew 20:1–16) 126

41. Investment—(Matthew 25:14–30) 129
42. The Good Samaritan—(Luke 10:25–37) 132
43. The Prodigal Son—(Luke 15:11–32) 135
44. The Persistent Widow—(Luke 18:1–8) 138
45. Pharisee & Tax Collector—(Luke 18:9–14) 140
46. The Triumphal Entry—(Luke 19:28–44) 143
47. Jesus Clears the Temple—(Mark 11:15–19) 146
48. Washing the Disciples' Feet—(John 13:1–17) 148
49. The Last Supper—(Matthew 26:20–30) 151
50. Jesus in Gethsemane—(Mark 14:32–42) 154

51. Jesus Arrested—(Matthew 26:47–56) 157
52. Peter Disowns Jesus—(Mark 14:66–72) 159
53. Jesus Before Pilate—(Mark 15:1–15) 161
54. Jesus' Crucifixion—(John 19:16–30) 164
55. Jesus' Resurrection—(Luke 24:1–12) 167
56. Jesus Appears to Mary Magdalene—(John 20:1–18) 169
57. On the Road to Emmaus—(Luke 24:13–35) 172
58. Jesus Appears to Thomas—(John 20:24–31) 175
59. Jesus Reinstates Peter—(John 21:15–25) 178
60. Jesus' Ascension & Great Commission 181
    (Acts 1:1–11; Matt. 28:16–20)

END NOTES 185

KEY WORDS 186

LEADER'S GUIDE FOR CELL GROUPS 194

 # START HERE

We tell stories,
    we watch stories,
        we live stories.

EVERYTHING BEGINS WITH STORY!

Typical small group Bible studies focus on learning content or memorizing a Bible section. That may work for individuals, but not for groups. Instead, these studies tap into how we best grow and learn.

Research shows us that:

⇨ EPIC STORIES[1] light up our entire brains. Impactful **episodes** help us to naturally remember things and to apply what we learn to future life situations. For example, think back to a major event in your life. You can remember amazing details—even colors and textures—from years past.[2]

⇨ SOCIAL VALUES (biblical values are social values—relating to God or humans) are learned through relationships in a **Cell Group community**. We may read about or hear teaching about biblical values, but they never become reality until practiced in a small, safe community. It's called **RELATIONAL Bible Study**.[3]

⇨ STUDY QUESTIONS must connect to our LEARNING PREFERENCES. Some of us want to know **WHY** we need to learn something. Others just want content—**WHAT** (Bible studies usually begin and end here, connecting to less than 20% of the group). Still others are more concerned with **HOW** to use what we're learning. Finally, some dream about **WHAT ELSE** we could do with what we learn.[4]

⇨ CELL-GROUP BIBLE STUDIES based around **STORY** help us "come to Jesus as a little child" (see Matthew 19:14). As children we can walk and dance into the scripture, in its context—viewing the scenes from all sorts of fresh and exciting angles. And chances are we will laugh, cry, and grow.[5]

⇨ CONNECTING THREE STORIES captures the best of the learning research—guiding us into the Bible.
  - The FIRST story is God's story (told through the Bible)—showing God's creative plan for humans, our walking away from God's plan, and God's becoming human (Jesus) to call us back home.

- The SECOND story is another person's life story, with all its stuff.
- The THIRD story is my story, with all of its stuff.

Remember, Jesus said that when two or three people gather in his name that he shows up (Matthew 18:20). We can count on that. When the three stories come together in a Cell Group, amazing things happen.

WHAT'S INSIDE?

This book captures 60 of the Epic Stories from the life of Jesus, found in the four Gospels (the Bible books of Matthew, Mark, Luke, and John).
It includes:

- The group session agendas for each story.
- Several different Bible translations. The authors chose the translation they felt gave the best interpretation and insight into the Epic Story. Feel free to use your mobile device to choose other translations for comparison.
- Many parallel references—where the same story is told by a different author. Again, you can do comparisons.

DID YOU SAY 60 SESSIONS?

Yes, but we only chose what we thought were the top 60 to get you started.

Most Cell Groups work together for about 6-8 weeks, then recommit to another 6-8 weeks. Plan to take a brief break after 6-8 weeks before starting again. This gives people opportunity to leave the group gracefully, or just catch their breath.

THE SESSION AGENDAS

EACH SESSION includes FIVE parts:
- BACK STORY—since we have pulled only the nuggets of each Epic Story out of the Bible, the Back Story gives the lead up and surrounding context.
- GATHERING (whole group)—about 15 minutes to welcome new people and set the stage for the session with an open-ended question or two. Make sure to have a beverage and snack ready.
- FINDING MY STORY IN GOD'S STORY (in groups of 3–5)—approximately 45 minutes to read the Bible story and answer questions; giving each person a chance to share a piece of their own story in the context of the Bible story.

- OUR STORY (whole group)—about 30 minutes for the entire group to care for one another, pray together, make new commitments, and reflect on the group work.
- IN BETWEEN (indivudually)—an assignment to complete before the next group session. A reminder to pray for and support one another, work on individual missions, and complete chosen commitments.

LIVING ON MISSION*

**Every group,
    every person,
        is called to mission!**

In the New Testament book of Ephesians, chapter 4, St. Paul summarizes how Jesus gifted the entire church to accomplish God's mission of renewing and restoring our world. And since each person is created with the image of God planted in them, we, as individuals—all of us, everyday normal people—are commissioned, and gifted, to live out Jesus' mission as part of the Church.

But that doesn't have to be a complicated, frightening experience. It means we have the opportunity to encourage and serve others in our "marketplace"—everyday moments, everyday locations—at work, at home, with neighbors, or at play. This is where our part in Jesus' mission becomes transformational to the world around us.

So, during these Epic studies, you will be encouraged to step out into your neighborhood on "mission," and report back the next week to your group.

ALSO, every group member should be looking for people who can join the group to fill an "empty chair." That's what keeps Cell Groups healthy and growing—new people whose stories are added to the stories of current group members.

**So, gather a few friends around your favorite table,
    in your favorite THIRD PLACE.**[6]
        **Open up this guide to the session agendas, and
            get started on a journey into these Epic Stories.**

1. You can do further reading by looking up "Episodic Declarative Memory."

2. Jessica Cruickshank—a demonstrated disciple-maker and facilitator of spiritual transformation. Jesse is an ordained Foursquare minister and a nationally recognized leader in the fields of experiential education and educational neuroscience. She holds a master's degree from Harvard University in Mind, Brain and Education. Jesse is passionate about creating organic systems that facilitate holistic human and organizational development.

3. Lev Vygotsky—a Russian psychologist (1896—1934) discovered that social values are best learned when experimented with (tried out) in social settings.

4. See Bernice McCarthy at About Learning, Inc., Wauconda, IL. Check out her The Learning Cycle, The 21st-Century and Millennial Learners (About Learning, 2012). ISBN: 978-1929040049. Available at AboutLearning.com or Amazon.com.

5. Dr. Lyman Coleman and Dr. Daryl L. Smith each have a lifetime of guiding life transformation in small, relational Bible study groups. They have also written extensively. Check out their many resources at Amazon.com.

6. If you're not familiar with the term, "Third Place" describes a welcoming place where people hang out with friends beyond their home (first place) and work (second place). It may be a pub, coffee shop, or wherever else you can share life with friends and family. The term was first coined by Ray Oldenburg in *The Great Good Place* (Cambridge: DaCapo Press, 1989).

---

* To discover more about living on mission as a group, you may read *Discovering Your Missional Potential: An Encounter with Ephesians 4 and How Jesus Lives It* by Daryl L. Smith & Andrew B. Smith (100 Movements, 2019). ISBN: 978-0-9986393-7-6

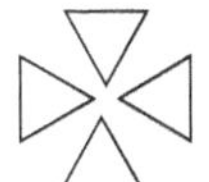

GROUP LEADER BASICS

[A more extensive **Leader's Guide** is posted at the back of this book.]

⇨ **CELL GROUP LEADERS** guide a small group of people (usually 5–12) on a journey to discover more about who Jesus is, how to become more like him, and serve on mission outside the group.

The idea of facilitating a Cell Group may be new and scary. You may have been pushed into this role. Someone may have challenged you into a stretching experiment. Or you may have been wondering how to grow your walk with Jesus to a deeper level. Whatever the scenario, just hang on and watch what happens in the weeks ahead!

⇨ **THE PRIMARY PURPOSE** of the Cell Group (consider using the term Village Group) is to help the group members ...
- Grow healthy relationships with God and one another,
- Discover Jesus' Kingdom plan through relational Bible study—connecting the three stories.
- Become equipped for vocational, missional living, and
- Launch into group and personal mission wherever they live, work, and play.

⇨ **A CHECKLIST**

The Cell Group Leader will:

☐ Guide the group sessions (topic, time usage, etc.); coordinating the start time and place for the group meetings with the group.

☐ Keep the group session on track, within the time limits. A group session should last about **1.5 hours**.

☐ START and STOP each session on time. If some want to continue with discussion after the scheduled conclusion time, dismiss everyone and let those who want to stay, stay. People will be energized for the next group session if they haven't felt trapped.

☐ **NOT** teach the Bible, but rather guide the group in discovery.

☐ **NOT** give advice, nor allow other group members to do so.

☐ Watch the time. You will not always be able to cover every question. When you must cut off discussion, it is important to give time signals (at least at the 5-minute and 2-minute points) before stopping.

You may hear some groans when time is cut short. Explain what you're doing—"keeping your word to end the session on time." The complaining means that discussion was going well.

☐ Make sure each person has a book, printout, or digital copy of the session materials.

☐ Ask people NOT to bring Bible commentaries or other books. The "official answer" will always shut down conversation.

☐ Respect each person and their opinions. As you model respect, people will see that differing opinions don't call for rudeness or demeaning behavior.

☐ Provide care for group members and their families between meetings. Encourage (have someone coordinate) the group members in their care for one another.

☐ Keep CONFIDENTIALITY. The group may only break confidence if a person is doing (or contemplating) something dangerous. Then you will tell the person that you are breaking confidence and must notify the appropriate authorities.

☐ Go FIRST in answering questions early in the group life. It helps to break the ice when you give an example of how you would answer. However, silence for thinking helps the introverts become equal contributors with the extroverts.

☐ Carefully note that each section of the AGENDA has a specific purpose. Depending on time, you may need to **skip some questions**; but be sure to include at least one question from each section. They are vital to everything that the group is about.

~ THE **EPIC** STORIES ~

CHECK THIS OUT!

Additional information about **bolded words** in the **BACK STORY** text (as well as other words) can be found in the END NOTES and KEY WORDS sections in the back of the book (beginning on page 186).

Asterisks (*) point to parallel story accounts in other parts of the New Testament.

1 THE BIRTH OF JESUS FORETOLD (LUKE 1:26-38)

☕ GATHER (all)

What details have you been told about the events surrounding your birth? Who told you about it?

"I was a big baby—more than 9 pounds! And I had brown eyes when I was born. Most babies are born with bluish eyes."

"My parents grew up in Michigan, but, when I was on the way, we lived in Columbus, Ohio. The states were huge college football rivals. The weekend I was born was the 'big game' in Columbus, so the hospital nurses put OSU balloons on my little cart and the OSU cheerleaders came to the maternity ward. Our family has laughed a lot about that over the years."

Read | Discuss Questions

[26]In the sixth month of Elizabeth's pregnancy, God sent the angel Gabriel to Nazareth, a village in Galilee, [27]to a virgin named Mary. She was engaged to be married to a man named Joseph, a descendant of King David. [28]Gabriel appeared to her and said, "Greetings, favored woman! The Lord is with you!"

[29]Confused and disturbed, Mary tried to think what the angel could mean. [30]"Don't be afraid, Mary," the angel told her, "for you have found favor with God! [31]You will conceive and give birth to a son, and you will name him Jesus. [32]He will be very great and will be called the Son of the Most High. The Lord God will give him the throne of his ancestor David. [33]And he will reign over Israel forever; his Kingdom will never end!"

[34]Mary asked the angel, "But how can this happen? I am a virgin."

[35]The angel replied, "The Holy Spirit will come upon you, and the power of the Most High will overshadow you. So the baby to be born will be holy, and he will be called the Son of God. [36]What's more, your relative Elizabeth has become pregnant in her old age! People used to say she was barren, but she has conceived a son and is now in her sixth month. [37]For the word of God will never fail."

[38]Mary responded, "I am the Lord's servant. May everything you have said about me come true." And then the angel left her.

—Luke 1:26–38 (NLT)

*Parallel account: Matthew 1:18-2:12.

BACK STORY*: Our story begins with a young girl being visited by an angelic being named **Gabriel** and told that she would be the mother of **Jesus**. Women in biblical times were often 12–14 years old when married. To be **engaged** was a binding commitment. Mary is a great-granddaughter of Israel's most famous **King—David**. Luke tells us some interesting things about who this baby is and will grow up to be. Mary's response is an amazing example of trusting God in the midst of a difficult situation; Jesus and his family would be taunted about the circumstances of his birth into his adulthood.

1. If you had been Mary, what would have been hardest to comprehend?
   - How is this being favored by God?
   - Getting pregnant as a virgin
   - Who this child really was
   - Explaining the pregnancy to Joseph and my family
   - Other _______________

2. What emotions do you think Mary felt about giving birth to the Messiah?
   - Scared to death
   - Honored
   - Burdened
   - Overjoyed
   - Clueless
   - All of the above
   - Other _______________

3. Why do you think the angel told Mary about Elizabeth's "condition"?
   - To prove God's power
   - To encourage her
   - To give her something else to think about
   - Other _______________

4. If an angel revealed God's plan for your life, what would you do first?

5. What about Jesus most gets your attention?
   - His conception—by the Holy Spirit and a virgin
   - His humanity—as a man who can relate to us
   - His authority—as an eternal king
   - His mission—as Savior (Jesus means "the Lord saves")
   - Other _______________

OUR STORY (all) 

6. How did you begin to understand who Jesus is, if your have?
   - It was an instantaneous insight.
   - It came over a long time.
   - I don't think I understand much of anything, yet.
   - Other _______________

7. What ONE gift did this group give you during this session?

8. How do you need this group to pray for you this week?

IN BETWEEN (individual)

Who might you encourage to fill the "empty chair" at the next group session?

2 MARY VISITS ELIZABETH (LUKE 1:39-56)

Who do you call FIRST when you have news to share?
Does it make a difference if it's good news or bad news?

Read | Discuss Questions

³⁹At that time Mary got ready and hurried to a town in the hill country of Judea, ⁴⁰where she entered Zechariah's home and greeted Elizabeth. ⁴¹When Elizabeth heard Mary's greeting, the baby leaped in her womb, and Elizabeth was filled with the Holy Spirit. ⁴²In a loud voice she exclaimed: "Blessed are you among women, and blessed is the child you will bear! ⁴³But why am I so favored, that the mother of my Lord should come to me? ⁴⁴As soon as the sound of your greeting reached my ears, the baby in my womb leaped for joy. ⁴⁵Blessed is she who has believed that the Lord would fulfill his promises to her!"

⁴⁶And Mary said:

"My soul glorifies the Lord
⁴⁷ and my spirit rejoices in God my Savior,
⁴⁸ for he has been mindful
　of the humble state of his servant.
　From now on all generations will call me blessed,
⁴⁹ for the Mighty One has done great things for me—holy is his name.
⁵⁰ His mercy extends to those who fear him, from generation to generation.
⁵¹ He has performed mighty deeds with his arm; he has scattered those who are proud in their inmost thoughts.
⁵² He has brought down rulers from their thrones but has lifted up the humble.
⁵³ He has filled the hungry with good things but has sent the rich away empty.
⁵⁴ He has helped his servant Israel, remembering to be merciful
⁵⁵ to Abraham and his descendants forever, just as he promised our ancestors."

⁵⁶Mary stayed with Elizabeth for about three months and then returned home.

—Luke 1:39–56 (NIV)

BACK STORY: In this Bible story, Mary hurries off to visit **Elizabeth** (a relative), who is pregnant with a miracle child of her own (later to be known as "John the Baptist"). **Zachariah**, Elizabeth's husband, was a Jewish priest. Luke (a doctor) tells us that when Mary approached, the baby jumped in Elizabeth's womb. In response to Elizabeth's comments, Mary expresses praise to God in a song. She speaks thanks for God's treatment, for God's mercy through the ages to all who trust in God, for God's power and provision, and for God's fulfillment of a promise made to Abraham ages ago (Genesis 12:1–3).

1. If this story was a movie script, and you were the director, what kind of music would you put in the background? Why?

2. Why do you think Mary went to Elizabeth's house?
    - For a little "female bonding"
    - To share her exciting news
    - To share in the joy of another pregnant woman
    - To get some advice from an older and wiser relative
    - To get away from the talk about her "illegitimate" pregnancy
    - Other _______________

3. Who in this story do you relate to most: Elizabeth, Mary, one of the fetal babies? Why?

4. As you "listen" to Mary's song, what impresses you most about her?
    - She came from a simple background.
    - She had a humble spirit.
    - She gave God the glory for her blessings.
    - She believed that the amazing prediction she heard would be accomplished.
    - She didn't let what others thought about her (being pregnant) control her.
    - Other _______________

5. How do you think Mary now viewed herself?
    - A lowly servant
    - A surrogate mother
    - An ordinary person
    - A woman who would now have a legacy
    - Other _______________

6. What about Mary and Elizabeth's relationship compares to your best friendship?
    - Shared their experiences
    - Took time to visit one other
    - Talked about their faith
    - Weren't competitive
    - Other _______________

OUR STORY (all) 

7. What do you need to share with an "Elizabeth" right now?
    - A joy I've been wanting to share
    - A burden I need to talk about
    - Some questions about my faith
    - Just a good time
    - Other _______________

8. How can this group help you take a next-best step with Jesus, this week? Make commitments among yourselves to connect this week.

IN BETWEEN (individual)

- Remember to follow through with your commitments from the group session.
- How can you begin to reach out with encouragement or service to someone near you (such as a neighbor, store clerk, waiter)?

3 AN ANGEL APPEARS TO JOSEPH (MATTHEW 1:18-25)

Choose one:

- What did your parents tell you about their courtship that is interesting or strange?

- Do you know how your parents picked your name? What does your name mean?

"My parents knew of each other growing up, but never actually got to know each other. They went to France through the same program and that's where they fell in love!"

"My dad was interested in my mom, but he wouldn't make a move. She decided to give him one last opportunity—at church. When she realized he'd left the building, she walked out ... only to meet him waiting for her. Evidently, after leaving, he decided if he was going to ask her out, he needed to do it then! Good thing! He almost missed his chance!"

Read | Discuss Questions

¹⁸Now the birth of Jesus Christ was as follows: After His mother Mary was betrothed to Joseph, before they came together, she was found with child of the Holy Spirit. ¹⁹Then Joseph her husband, being a just man, and not wanting to make her a public example, was minded to put her away secretly. ²⁰But while he thought about these things, behold, an angel of the Lord appeared to him in a dream, saying, "Joseph, son of David, do not be afraid to take to you Mary your wife, for that which is conceived in her is of the Holy Spirit. ²¹And she will bring forth a Son, and you shall call His name Jesus, for He will save His people from their sins."

²²So all this was done that it might be fulfilled which was spoken by the Lord through the prophet, saying: ²³"Behold, the virgin shall be with child, and bear a Son, and they shall call His name Immanuel," which is translated, "God with us."

²⁴Then Joseph, being aroused from sleep, did as the angel of the Lord commanded him and took to him his wife, ²⁵and did not know her till she had brought forth her firstborn Son. And he called His name Jesus.

—Matthew 1:18–25 (NKJV)

BACK STORY: Joseph, **engaged** to Mary, learns of her pregnancy—more than likely from Mary before she leaves to visit Elizabeth and await his response. In Matthew 1:1–17, we read Jesus' (and therefore Joseph's) genealogy all the way back to Abraham, and find that they are all descendants of **King David**. As Joseph is about to quietly (rather than publicly) divorce Mary, an angel speaks to him about this unexpected pregnancy. (A Jewish engagement could only be broken by a divorce.) Joseph changes his mind and goes ahead with the wedding.

1. Assuming Mary was the one who told YOU (her future husband) she was pregnant, what would you have thought first?
   - There must be some other guy.
   - That's it; we're through!
   - She's never lied to me before—maybe she's telling the truth.
   - Surely God has a big plan in mind.
   - Other _______________________

2. Do you think this mysterious pregnancy more strained or strengthened Joseph and Mary's future marriage relationship? Why?

3. Who was your most significant role model when you were a teenager?
   - My father
   - My mother
   - A relative or family friend
   - A sports figure/coach/teacher
   - A church leader
   - Other _______________________

4. Jesus was called Immanuel—"God with us." How might he be a role model for you?
   - His divine nature makes him too different from me.
   - His divine nature makes him the ultimate role model.
   - He's the Savior, not a role model.
   - Other _______________________

5. If he did, when did Jesus become a warm person to you—more than just a name?
   - Several years ago
   - When I gave my life to him as a child or youth
   - Only recently
   - I'm just beginning to see who Jesus is.
   - I'm not at that point yet.
   - Other _______________________

OUR STORY (all) 

6. What new understanding have you discovered about Jesus during the time in this group today?

7. What big question do you still have, that you'd like to ask Jesus about?

8. How would you like this group to pray for you, before the next meeting?

IN BETWEEN (individual)

- Remember to pray for the other group members, remembering the specific requests they mentioned at the last meeting.
- What opportunities are you looking for, to encourage or serve where you live, work, or play?

THE BIRTH OF JESUS
(LUKE 2:1-20)

GATHER (all)

Choose one:

- Were you ever in a Christmas program or any drama? What part did you play?

- Parents: What was your reaction when you found out you were going to have your first baby?

Were you ever in a Christmas program or any drama?

"Now there were in the same country shep-herds living out in the fields, keeping watch over their flock by night ...."

Read | Discuss Questions

¹⁻⁵About that time Caesar Augustus ordered a census to be taken throughout the Empire. This was the first census when Quirinius was governor of Syria. Everyone had to travel to his own ancestral hometown to be accounted for. So Joseph went from the Galilean town of Nazareth up to Bethlehem in Judah, David's town, for the census. As a descendant of David, he had to go there. He went with Mary, his fiancée, who was pregnant.

⁶⁻⁷While they were there, the time came for her to give birth. She gave birth to a son, her firstborn. She wrapped him in a blanket and laid him in a manger, because there was no room in the hostel.

⁸⁻¹²There were sheepherders camping in the neighborhood. They had set night watches over their sheep. Suddenly, God's angel stood among them and God's glory blazed around them. They were terrified. The angel said, "Don't be afraid. I'm here to announce a great and joyful event that is meant for everybody, worldwide: A Savior has just been born in David's town, a Savior who is Messiah and Master. This is what you're to look for: a baby wrapped in a blanket and lying in a manger."

¹³⁻¹⁴At once the angel was joined by a huge angelic choir singing God's praises:
Glory to God in the heavenly heights,
Peace to all men and women on earth who please him.

¹⁵⁻¹⁸As the angel choir withdrew into heaven, the sheepherders talked it over. "Let's get over to Bethlehem as fast as we can and see for ourselves what God has revealed to us." They left, running, and found Mary and Joseph, and the baby lying in the manger. Seeing was believing. They told everyone they met what the angels had said about this child. All who heard the sheepherders were impressed.

¹⁹⁻²⁰Mary kept all these things to herself, holding them dear, deep within herself. The sheepherders returned and let loose, glorifying and praising God for everything they had heard and seen. It turned out exactly the way they'd been told!

—Luke 2:1–20 (MSG)

BACK STORY: Christianity is no fairy tale. Luke goes to great lengths to link his biblical story to known historical times and figures. Jesus was born when **Augustus** was emperor of Rome and Publius Sulpicius **Quirinius** was in Syria. Roman records detail the practice of "registration" for the purpose of administering taxes to support the empire. Joseph, who was living in Nazareth, being a descendant of King David, had to return to Bethlehem, David's home town.

Luke records three titles for the baby who would bring Good News: **Savior, Christ,** and **Lord.** Angels are the first to announce Jesus' birth as they appear to a group of shepherds on a hill outside Bethlehem.

1. Imagine that you were sent by *The Bethlehem Gazette* to cover this "New Christmas baby" story. What part of the story would you want to photograph first?

2. From this brief account, what most impresses you about Mary and Joseph?
   - They were dutiful citizens.
   - They were related to the famous King David.
   - They were humble.
   - They kept going in the tough times.
   - Other _______________

3. If you had been in Mary and Joseph's shoes (not able to find a room), what would you have done?
   - Gone back home
   - Had a good cry
   - Taken it out on my spouse
   - Prayed for God's provision
   - Other _______________

4. From what you know about the shepherds in that time, why do you think God chose to announce Jesus' birth to them?
   - They were the only people who were close by.
   - They needed some hope.
   - They were close to God.
   - They were an example of the people that Jesus came for.
   - Other _______________

OUR STORY (all) 

5. How has the news of Christ's birth impacted you?
   - I don't think it has yet.
   - It's awakened a sense of joy.
   - It gives me hope for the future.
   - It's just made me more confused about God's plan for me.
   - Other _______________

6. After discussing this story, what message from an "angel" would you like to hear today?

7. Who in the group has given you the "gift of listening" today?

8. Where are you going to serve or encourage one "invisible person" in your life this week?

IN BETWEEN (individual)

- Remember to support one another in prayer.
- Remember your commitment to serve or encourage the "invisible person."

5 JESUS PRESENTED AT THE TEMPLE (LUKE 2:21-40)

GATHER (all)

Choose one:

- If you could retire anywhere in the world, where would you live?

- What is the most unusual religious service you've ever attended?

FINDING MY STORY in GOD'S STORY
(groups of 3–5)

Read | Discuss Questions

21And when eight days were completed for the circumcision of the Child, His name was called Jesus, the name given by the angel before He was conceived in the womb. Jesus Presented in the Temple.
22Now when the days of her purification according to the law of Moses were completed, they brought Him to Jerusalem to present Him to the Lord 23(as it is written in the law of the Lord, "Every male who opens the womb shall be called holy to the Lord"), 24and to offer a sacrifice according to what is said in the law of the Lord, "A pair of turtledoves or two young pigeons." 25And behold, there was a man in Jerusalem whose name was Simeon, and this man was just and devout, waiting for the Consolation of Israel, and the Holy Spirit was upon him. 26And it had been revealed to him by the Holy Spirit that he would not see death before he had seen the Lord's Christ. 27So he came by the Spirit into the temple. And when the parents brought in the Child Jesus, to do for Him according to the custom of the law, 28he took Him up in his arms and blessed God and said:
29"Lord, now You are letting Your servant depart in peace,
According to Your word;
30For my eyes have seen Your salvation
31Which You have prepared before the face of all peoples,

[32]A light to bring revelation to the Gentiles,
And the glory of Your people Israel."
[33]And Joseph and His mother marveled at those things which were spoken of Him. [34]Then Simeon blessed them, and said to Mary His mother, "Behold, this Child is destined for the fall and rising of many in Israel, and for a sign which will be spoken against [35](yes, a sword will pierce through your own soul also), that the thoughts of many hearts may be revealed."

[36]Now there was one, Anna, a prophetess, the daughter of Phanuel, of the tribe of Asher. She was of a great age, and had lived with a husband seven years from her virginity; [37]and this woman was a widow of about eighty-four years, who did not depart from the temple, but served God with fastings and prayers night and day. [38]And coming in that instant she gave thanks to the Lord, and spoke of Him to all those who looked for redemption in Jerusalem.

[39]So when they had performed all things according to the law of the Lord, they returned to Galilee, to their own city, Nazareth. [40]And the Child grew and became strong in spirit, filled with wisdom; and the grace of God was upon Him.

—Luke 2:21–40 (NKJV)

BACK STORY: In this story, Mary and Joseph fulfill three legal requirements for Jewish parents: circumcision, ritual purification of the mother, and dedication (consecration) of the firstborn. Luke records the testimony of two eye witnesses at the presentation of Jesus to the Priest in the Temple—Simeon and Anna. In their words are hints that Jesus' mission would be not only for the Jews, but also for the **Gentile** (non-Jewish) world. Simeon's comments allude to the more difficult impact of Jesus' ministry.

---

1. If you could have been either Simeon or Anna, which would you choose? Why?

2. What do you most admire about Simeon and Anna, from this story?
   - Hanging out in the temple for so many years
   - Their devotion to God
   - Their belief that this child was actually the Messiah
   - They had lived a really long time
   - Other _______________________

3. If you were Joseph or Mary, how would you title your diary entry to describe this day?
   - "Creepy people showed up at Jesus' dedication."
   - "Everybody loves him—I am so proud!"
   - "Old people say such strange things sometimes!"
   - "I've never had so much to thank God for."
   - "What did that man mean about a sword piercing my soul?"
   - Other _______________________

4. How would you describe your parents' help in maturing spiritually?
    - It never crossed their minds.
    - They took me to church.
    - I wish they had prayed with me.
    - They told me about Jesus.
    - Other _______________________

5. What would be the biggest joy for you, in your old age?
    - To see my grandchildren
    - To see my family serving God
    - To leave the world a better place
    - To feel I have done God's will
    - Other _______________________

6. This story shows us that God had a plan for Jesus' life. What question would you most like to ask God about the plan/purpose for your life?
    - I'm not sure what I'd ask.
    - I want to know the plan, NOW!
    - I don't want to know ahead of time.
    - How can I make a difference in this world?
    - Other _______________________

OUR STORY (all) 

7. Report in from your attempt to bless, encourage or serve an "invisible person" last week. What was the response from the person you blessed?

8. How might God want you to "bless" a person this coming week?
    - Meaningful gift
    - Card or letter
    - Call or text
    - Personal visit
    - My time
    - Prayer
    - Other _______________________

9. How can this group pray for you and that person you want to bless?

IN BETWEEN (individual)

Plan to start your "blessing" early in the week, so you don't miss the opportunity. Listen closely to how they respond ("behind their words" to what they really mean). Think of ways you can further encourage them.

NOTES/COMMENTS

6 YOUNG JESUS AT THE TEMPLE (LUKE 2:41-52)

Choose one:

- As a child, when were you lost or separated from your parent or guardian? OR when have you lost a child (or discovered they were hiding from you)?

- If you turned up missing now, where's the first place your family would look for you? The last place?

📖 **FINDING MY STORY in GOD'S STORY** (groups of 3–5)

Read | Discuss Questions

[41]Every year Jesus' parents went to Jerusalem for the Festival of the Passover. [42]When he was twelve years old, they went up to the festival, according to the custom. [43]After the festival was over, while his parents were returning home, the boy Jesus stayed behind in Jerusalem, but they were unaware of it. [44]Thinking he was in their company, they traveled on for a day. Then they began looking for him among their relatives and friends. [45]When they did not find him, they went back to Jerusalem to look for him. [46]After three days they found him in the temple courts, sitting among the teachers, listening to them and asking them questions.

[47]Everyone who heard him was amazed at his understanding and his answers. [48]When his parents saw him, they were astonished. His mother said to him, "Son, why have you treated us like this? Your father and I have been anxiously searching for you."

[49]"Why were you searching for me?" he asked. "Didn't you know I had to be in my Father's house?" [50]But they did not understand what he was saying to them.

[51]Then he went down to Nazareth with them and was obedient to them. But his mother treasured all these things in her heart. [52]And Jesus grew in wisdom and stature, and in favor with God and man.

—Luke 2:41–52 (NIV)

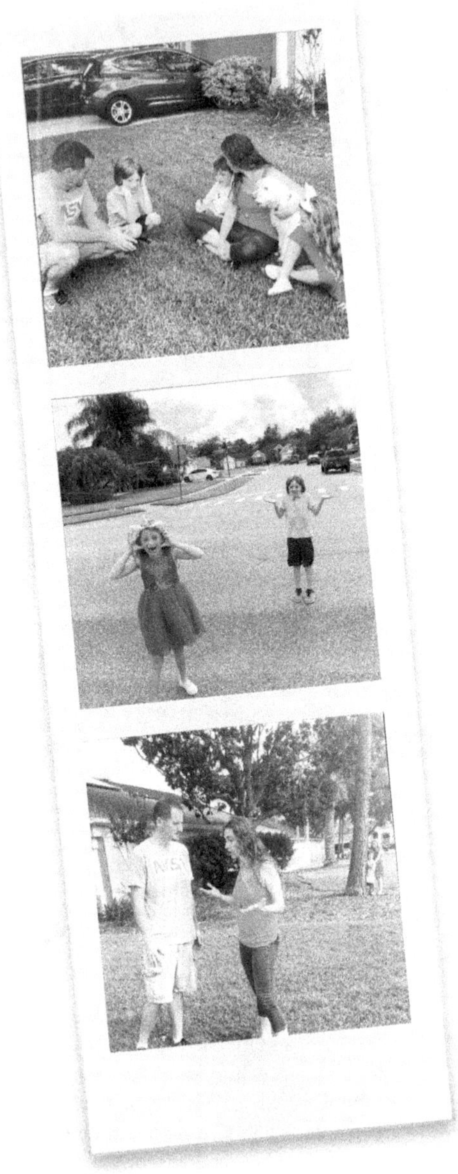

BACK STORY: Luke gives us the only account, in the Protestant Bible, of Jesus' life between his infancy and adulthood. Like other devout Jews, Mary, Joseph, and 12-year-old Jesus have traveled to Jerusalem for one of the historic Jewish **feasts** (Passover). Jewish pilgrims traveled in large caravans. Typically, the women and children would be up front while the men and older boys came along behind. At the end of the day's travel, Jesus was not found anywhere in the caravan. A panicked Mary and Joseph return to Jerusalem to find Jesus amazing the teachers in the temple courts with his knowledge and the questions he asks.

1. What surprised you most about 12-year-old Jesus' behavior in this story?
   - He acted like most 12-year-olds, not understanding his parents' fear.
   - His ability to talk with adult leaders
   - Not even realizing he'd been left behind
   - His willingness to go home with his parents
   - Other ___________________

2. If you had been Mary or Joseph, how would you have reacted when you discovered Jesus was missing?
   - Called 911
   - Cried and panicked
   - Gone into shock
   - Blamed my spouse
   - Figured he would show up
   - Other ___________________

3. What would you have done when you finally found Jesus?
   - Cried and given him a hug
   - Yelled at him about taking responsibility
   - Let him explain himself
   - Grounded him for a month
   - Other ___________________

4. What insight do you get from this story about young Jesus?
   - He knew he was God's Son.
   - He was independent.
   - He had knowledge and understanding.
   - He still had some growing up to do.
   - Other ___________________

5. As you grew up, when did you feel you weren't a kid anymore?
   - Working a summer job
   - Getting a driver's license
   - Starting middle school
   - Other ___________________

6. How does this story connect to YOU?
   - Even Jesus' parents had to go through stress and challenges.
   - Jesus did things that worried his parents.
   - Everyone needs a chance to grow up.
   - Developing independence is important for maturity.
   - Other ___________________

7. Where do you need to focus attention in growing a relationship with God?

OUR STORY (all) 

8. How did the "blessing another person" go this week? What did you learn from them?

9. How can this group pray for you now and in the coming week?

IN BETWEEN (individual)

Look for a new person in your neighborhood to introduce yourself to.

7 THE BAPTISM & TEMPTATION OF JESUS (MATTHEW 3:13-4:11)

 **GATHER** (all)

Choose one:

- What gets you through a time of confinement?

- What are you tempted by that is either fattening or expensive?

What gets you through a time of [[CONFINEMENT]] ?

Read | Discuss Questions

¹³Then Jesus went from Galilee to the Jordan River to be baptized by John. ¹⁴But John tried to talk him out of it. "I am the one who needs to be baptized by you," he said, "so why are you coming to me?"

¹⁵But Jesus said, "It should be done, for we must carry out all that God requires." So John agreed to baptize him.

¹⁶After his baptism, as Jesus came up out of the water, the heavens were opened and he saw the Spirit of God descending like a dove and settling on him. ¹⁷And a voice from heaven said, "This is my dearly loved Son, who brings me great joy."

¹Then Jesus was led by the Spirit into the wilderness to be tempted there by the devil. ²For forty days and forty nights he fasted and became very hungry.

³During that time the devil[c] came and said to him, "If you are the Son of God, tell these stones to become loaves of bread."

⁴But Jesus told him, "No! The Scriptures say,
'People do not live by bread alone, but by every word that comes from the mouth of God.'"

⁵Then the devil took him to the holy city, Jerusalem, to the highest point of the Temple, ⁶and said, "If you are the Son of God, jump off! For the Scriptures say,
'He will order his angels to protect you.
And they will hold you up with their hands so you won't even hurt your foot on a stone.'"

⁷Jesus responded, "The Scriptures also say, 'You must not test the Lord your God.'"

⁸Next the devil took him to the peak of a very high mountain and showed him all the kingdoms of the world and their glory. ⁹"I will give it all to you," he said, "if you will kneel down and worship me."

¹⁰"Get out of here, Satan," Jesus told him. "For the Scriptures say,
'You must worship the Lord your God and serve only him.'"

¹¹Then the devil went away, and angels came and took care of Jesus.

—Matthew 3:13–17; 4:1–11 (NLT)

BACK STORY*: Here Matthew moves from Jesus' birth to his adulthood (he is now at least 30) and the beginning of his ministry as a **rabbi**. Jesus' public ministry is inaugurated with baptism by his cousin John (the Baptist) and his temptation by Satan to mistrust God and misuse his power. Early in the Genesis creation story, Adam and Eve are tempted to mistrust God when the serpent misquotes God. Even in their perfect environment, they fail the test. Jesus, at his weakest, in a desert environment, uses Old Testament passages to correct and counter Satan's misuse of God's word—and emerges victorious.

*Parallel accounts: Luke 3:21-4:13; Mark 1:9ff

1. Why do you think God affirmed Jesus at his baptism? (3:16–17)
   - So the crowd would believe his teaching
   - To prove the skeptics wrong
   - He needed it just like anyone else
   - Other _______________

2. If you could have interviewed Jesus as he came out of the water, what BIG question would you have asked?

3. How vulnerable do you think Jesus was to the temptations?
   - Being so hungry and weak, he was really vulnerable.
   - He was as vulnerable as I am.
   - He wasn't vulnerable…he was God.
   - He was just trying to put the devil in his place.
   - I don't know if he was vulnerable, but this was God helping him grow up.
   - Other _______________

4. What event in your life helps define when you "grew up"?
   - Graduation
   - Leaving home
   - Starting a real job
   - Marriage
   - Other _______________

5. If the devil targeted you for temptation to do something you knew you shouldn't, which part of your life would he focus on?
   - Physical temptations
   - Financial areas
   - Ambition/power
   - My self-identity
   - My relationships
   - Other _______________

6. When do you find yourself most vulnerable to temptation?
   - When I'm tired or under stress
   - When I'm alone
   - After a spiritual high
   - When I'm not expecting it
   - Other _______________

7. When you look at how Jesus handled temptation, what might you learn, and use, the next time you're tempted?

OUR STORY (all) 

8. What or who has helped you during this session, in better understanding temptation?

9. How can the group pray for you, especially in the area of temptation?

IN BETWEEN (individual)

Be alert to temptations that might come your way this week. Jot notes in a journal of how you dealt with them.

8 WATER TO WINE (JOHN 2:1-12)

 **GATHER** (all)

What is the most unusual wedding you've ever attended or seen on TV?

FINDING MY STORY in GOD'S STORY (groups of 3–5)

Read | Discuss Questions

¹The next day there was a wedding celebration in the village of Cana in Galilee. Jesus' mother was there, ²and Jesus and his disciples were also invited to the celebration. ³The wine supply ran out during the festivities, so Jesus' mother told him, "They have no more wine." ⁴"Dear woman, that's not our problem," Jesus replied. "My time has not yet come." ⁵But his mother told the servants, "Do whatever he tells you." ⁶Standing nearby were six stone water jars, used for Jewish ceremonial washing. Each could hold twenty to thirty gallons. ⁷Jesus told the servants, "Fill the jars with water." When the jars had been filled, ⁸he said, "Now dip some out, and take it to the master of ceremonies." So the servants followed his instructions. ⁹When the master of ceremonies tasted the water that was now wine, not knowing where it had come from (though, of course, the servants knew), he called the bridegroom over.

¹⁰"A host always serves the best wine first," he said. "Then, when everyone has had a lot to drink, he brings out the less expensive wine. But you have kept the best until now!" ¹¹This miraculous sign at Cana in Galilee was the first time Jesus revealed his glory. And his disciples believed in him.

¹²After the wedding he went to Capernaum for a few days with his mother, his brothers, and his disciples.

—John 2:1–12 (NLT)

1. What is your first reaction to this story? Why?
   - I wish Jesus had been at my wedding!
   - It looks like Jesus was hassled by his mother, too.
   - I have a hard time picturing Jesus in a setting like this.
   - I find it odd that Jesus' first miracle had to do with wine.
   - Other ______________________

2. How do you think Jesus felt about his mother setting him up like this, in front of his new disciples?
   - Annoyed
   - Embarrassed
   - Honored
   - Manipulated
   - Awkward
   - Other ______________________

3. If you had been the wedding caterer, how would you have felt when you heard that someone brought in more and better wine?
   - Relieved—that was a close call!
   - Frustrated—there go my tips.
   - Embarrassed—I should have planned better.
   - Delighted—and I didn't have to pay for it.
   - Other ______________________

4. Where is the "wine level" (zest for living) in your life right now?
   - Overflowing
   - Half-full
   - I don't know
   - Running out fast
   - Empty
   - Other ______________________

BACK STORY: This Bible story is about a wedding celebration where Jesus performed his first miracle (turning water into wine). Weddings in Jesus' time were major events, lasting up to a week! Running out of wine was a social embarrassment. Mary reports the situation to Jesus and, after what may have looked like a rebuke, instructs the servant to do whatever he tells them. The water pots would have been there for washing the guests' feet. (An action that was refreshing as well as a means of cleaning off the road dirt.) This incident marks the beginning of a turning point for the disciples.

What is the most unusual wedding you've attended?

---

5. If Jesus could create "new wine" in your life, where would you need it most?

6. What next step would you like to take, in getting your "wine-level" back up?

OUR STORY (all) 

7. Complete the sentence: "This story makes me feel like _____________."

8. How can this group support you this week?

IN BETWEEN (individual)

- Spend time this week asking God to help you in your next step toward replenishing your "wine level." Try to write down two helpful ideas that come to your mind.
- Keep looking for people you can serve or encourage, where you live, work, or play.

9 JESUS TEACHES NICODEMUS (JOHN 3:1-21)

 **GATHER** (all)

Where were you born?

What is ONE important thing a tourist should know about that place?

"I was born in Kentucky. Kentucky is famous for horse racing, fried chicken, bluegrass music, and college basketball. (I know you just wanted one fact!)"

BACK STORY: Nicodemus, a man of some significance (a **Pharisee** and a **ruler of the Jews**), arrives after sunset seeking to learn more about **Rabbi** Jesus' teachings. Jesus engages him in a dialogue that boggles his mind with talk of rebirth, wind, Spirit, **snakes**, and the means of entering God's Kingdom. The miracles and teaching of Jesus had already convinced Nicodemus that Jesus is from God. Pharisees were one of four groups in Judaism of Jesus' day. As a ruler of the Jews he was one of the members of the Sanhedrin that acted as the civil and religious authority in Israel under the rule of the Romans.

Read |Discuss Questions

¹⁻²There was a man of the Pharisee sect, Nicodemus, a prominent leader among the Jews. Late one night he visited Jesus and said, "Rabbi, we all know you're a teacher straight from God. No one could do all the God-pointing, God-revealing acts you do if God weren't in on it."

³Jesus said, "You're absolutely right. Take it from me: Unless a person is born from above, it's not possible to see what I'm pointing to—to God's kingdom."

⁴"How can anyone," said Nicodemus, "be born who has already been born and grown up? You can't re-enter your mother's womb and be born again. What are you saying with this 'born-from-above' talk?"

⁵⁻⁶Jesus said, "You're not listening. Let me say it again. Unless a person submits to this original creation—the 'wind-hovering-over-the-water' creation, the invisible moving the visible, a baptism into a new life—it's not possible to enter God's kingdom. When you look at a baby, it's just that: a body you can look at and touch. But the person who takes shape within is formed by something you can't see and touch—the Spirit—and becomes a living spirit.

⁷⁻⁸"So don't be so surprised when I tell you that you have to be 'born from above'—out of this world, so to speak. You know well enough how the wind blows this way and that. You hear it rustling through the trees, but you have no idea where it comes from or where it's headed next. That's the way it is with everyone 'born from above' by the wind of God, the Spirit of God."

⁹Nicodemus asked, "What do you mean by this? How does this happen?"

¹⁰⁻¹²Jesus said, "You're a respected teacher of Israel and you don't know these basics? Listen carefully. I'm speaking sober truth to you. I speak only of what I know by experience; I give witness only to what I have seen with my own eyes. There is nothing secondhand here, no hearsay. Yet instead of facing the evidence and accepting it, you procrastinate with questions. If I tell you things that are plain as the hand before your face and you don't believe me, what use is there in telling you of things you can't see, the things of God?

¹³⁻¹⁵"No one has ever gone up into the presence of God except the One who came down from that Presence, the Son of Man. In the same way that Moses lifted the serpent in the desert so people could have something to see and then believe, it is necessary for the Son of Man to be lifted up—and everyone who looks up to him, trusting and expectant, will gain a real life, eternal life.

¹⁶⁻¹⁸"This is how much God loved the world: He gave his Son, his one and only Son. And this is why: so that no one need be destroyed; by believing in him, anyone can have a whole and lasting life. God didn't go to all the trouble of sending his Son merely to point an accusing finger, telling the world how bad it was. He came to help, to put the world right again. Anyone who trusts in him is acquitted; anyone who refuses to trust him has long since been under the death sentence without knowing it. And why? Because of that person's failure to believe in the one-of-a-kind Son of God when introduced to him.

¹⁹⁻²¹"This is the crisis we're in: God-light streamed into the world, but men and women everywhere ran for the darkness. They went for the darkness because they were not really interested in pleasing God. Everyone who makes a practice of doing evil, addicted to denial and illusion, hates God-light and won't come near it, fearing a painful exposure. But anyone working and living in truth and reality welcomes God-light so the work can be seen for the God-work it is."

—Luke 2:1–20 (MSG)

1. What would have been the most exciting part of eaves-dropping on this discussion?

2. Why do you think Nicodemus came to Jesus at night?
   - He had a day job.
   - It was the only time on Jesus schedule.
   - He was afraid of being seen by his friends.
   - Other _______________

3. Who does Nicodemus remind you of?
   - A philosophy student
   - A misguided "religious" person
   - A friend of mine
   - Myself
   - Other _______________

4. What do you think Jesus meant by "Unless you are born from above, it's not possible to see what I'm pointing to—to God's kingdom"?
   - To understand what God is up to, we must have God's help.
   - This relationship with God (Jesus) is supernatural-spiritual.
   - Our spiritual lives have a beginning, just like our physical lives.
   - A "new-life-birth" connects us to God's original plan for us.
   - Other _______________

5. What follow-up question(s) might you want to ask Jesus when Nicodemus left?

6. What is the most important point in this passage for you right now?
   - Like Nicodemus, it's ok for me to have questions.
   - I think I'm beginning to understand what Jesus wants from me.
   - I need to be born spiritually.
   - This story affirms how I've been trying to live.
   - This story gives me hope.
   - Other _______________

OUR STORY (all) 

7. What gift of "thanks" would you like to give someone in the group, today? Why?
8. Where do you need the group to help you take a next step toward a life with Jesus?
9. Who did you encourage or serve last week?

IN BETWEEN (individual)

- Re-read John 3:1–21 two or three times this week. Write down any new thoughts that come to your mind about growing in a walk with Jesus.
- Share what you're learning with one person.

10 JESUS & THE SAMARITAN WOMAN (JOHN 4:7-30)

 **GATHER** (all)

As a teenager, what was your favorite "watering hole" to hang out at?

"Our favorite spot was a pizza shop near the high school."

FINDING MY STORY in GOD'S STORY (groups of 3–5)

Read | Discuss Questions

———————————————

[7]Soon a Samaritan woman came to draw water, and Jesus said to her, "Please give me a drink." [8]He was alone at the time because his disciples had gone into the village to buy some food.
[9]The woman was surprised, for Jews refuse to have anything to do with Samaritans. She said to Jesus, "You are a Jew, and I am a Samaritan woman. Why are you asking me for a drink?"
[10]Jesus replied, "If you only knew the gift God has for you and who you are speaking to, you would ask me, and I would give you living water."

[11]"But sir, you don't have a rope or a bucket," she said, "and this well is very deep. Where would you get this living water? [12]And besides, do you think you're greater than our ancestor Jacob, who gave us this well? How can you offer better water than he and his sons and his animals enjoyed?"
[13]Jesus replied, "Anyone who drinks this water will soon become thirsty again. [14]But those who drink the water I give will never be thirsty again. It becomes a fresh, bubbling spring within them, giving them eternal life."
[15]"Please, sir," the woman said, "give me this water! Then I'll never be thirsty again,

and I won't have to come here to get water."
¹⁶"Go and get your husband," Jesus told her.
¹⁷"I don't have a husband," the woman replied.

Jesus said, "You're right! You don't have a husband— ¹⁸for you have had five husbands, and you aren't even married to the man you're living with now. You certainly spoke the truth!"
¹⁹"Sir," the woman said, "you must be a prophet. ²⁰So tell me, why is it that you Jews insist that Jerusalem is the only place of worship, while we Samaritans claim it is here at Mount Gerizim, where our ancestors worshiped?"
²¹Jesus replied, "Believe me, dear woman, the time is coming when it will no longer matter whether you worship the Father on this mountain or in Jerusalem. ²²You Samaritans know very little about the one you worship, while we Jews know all about him, for salvation comes through the Jews. ²³But the time is coming—indeed it's here now— when true worshipers will worship the Father in spirit and in truth. The Father is looking for those who will worship him that way. ²⁴For God is Spirit, so those who worship him must worship in spirit and in truth."
²⁵The woman said, "I know the Messiah is coming—the one who is called Christ. When he comes, he will explain everything to us."
²⁶Then Jesus told her, "I am the Messiah!"
²⁷Just then his disciples came back. They were shocked to find him talking to a woman, but none of them had the nerve to ask, "What do you want with her?" or "Why are you talking to her?" ²⁸The woman left her water jar beside the well and ran back to the village, telling everyone, ²⁹"Come and see a man who told me everything I ever did! Could he possibly be the Messiah?" ³⁰So the people came streaming from the village to see him.

—John 4:7–30 (NLT)

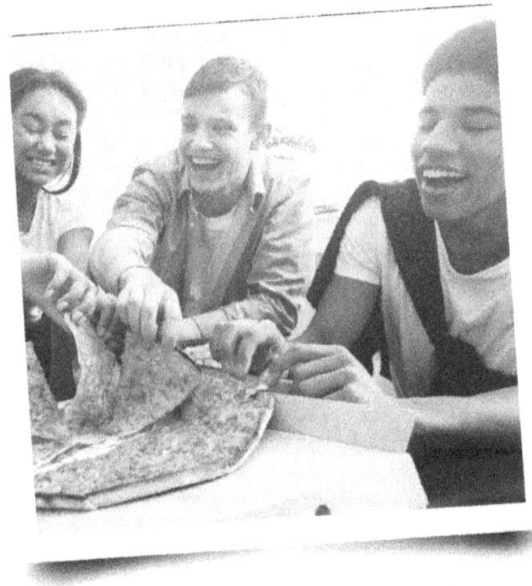

BACK STORY: Rather than avoid **Samaria**, as Jews often did, Jesus not only ventured in, but also stopped to talk with a woman—who turns out to be of questionable reputation. The "sixth hour" was twelve noon. The time and setting strongly suggest that she was not welcomed by the respectable women in this village who would fetch water much later in the day. Historical sources indicate that Jewish rabbis at that time disapproved of persons married more than three times. Jacob was the grandson of the Jewish patriarch, Abraham.

1. Put yourself in this woman's sandals. What would you have done when Jesus strode up to your well?
   - Run and hid
   - Said, "Let's have a party!"
   - Wondered how I was going to talk myself out of this situation
   - Other _______________

2. What most impresses you with this woman's response to Jesus?
   - Her openness and honesty
   - Her understanding of their ethnic differences
   - Her knowledge of spiritual truths
   - Her willingness to gain new insights
   - Other _______________

3. What most impresses you about Jesus intentionally going through Samaria and encountering this amazing woman?

4. Jesus offered this woman "living water." What do you think she really wanted?
   - Intimacy in her relationships
   - To know God better
   - Acceptance of who she was
   - Forgiveness
   - Other _______________

5. This woman expressed her thirst. What "thirst" would you most like Jesus to begin quenching in your life today?
   - For close friendships
   - For closeness with God
   - For acceptance of who I am
   - For forgiveness
   - For meaning/purpose in life
   - For basic survival in life
   - Other _______________

6. How might you start to get your thirst quenched?

OUR STORY (all) 

7. Jesus broke social and cultural norms to connect with this woman—and the town was changed. How might we overcome barriers to help change our world?
   - Initiate conversations with people different than us
   - Visit a part of town I've never been in before
   - Ask Jesus to help me see people as he does
   - Listen-to-learn from someone who has a different background
   - Other _______________

8. Which one of the above will you attempt this week, with Jesus' help?

   Take time to pray for one another as you're stretched this week to live like Jesus.

IN BETWEEN (individual)

This can be a great but stretching week as you attempt to break down barriers of difference. Look for a place you can sit and listen to people who talk, act, or live differently than you. What amazing things can you learn from them?

11 JESUS REJECTED IN NAZARETH (LUKE 4:14-30)

☕ GATHER (all)

When have you received a "Dear John" or rejection letter?

What was it for?

"I got turned down for a job that I thought was a lock. I was totally qualified—and really excited about working for that company. But they hired somone else."

BACK STORY: Early in Jesus' ministry, he shows up at the synagogue in Nazareth (where he grew up). Though he regularly attended services, on this day Jesus takes a turn reading the scripture portion—from Isaiah. Following the pattern of synagogue worship, he stands to read and then sits, as was the custom of a **rabbi**, to offer commentary on the passage. What he says, however, stirs up considerable controversy, gets him thrown out of town, and an attempt is made on his life. Did you know that some of the best-known passages of the Bible and classical music are found in the book of Isaiah?

Read | Discuss Questions

[14]Then Jesus returned in the power of the Spirit to Galilee, and news of Him went out through all the surrounding region. [15]And He taught in their synagogues, being glorified by all.

[16]So He came to Nazareth, where He had been brought up. And as His custom was, He went into the synagogue on the Sabbath day, and stood up to read. [17]And He was handed the book of the prophet Isaiah. And when He had opened the book, He found the place where it was written:

[18]"The Spirit of the Lord is upon Me,
Because He has anointed Me
To preach the gospel to the poor;
He has sent Me to heal the brokenhearted,
To proclaim liberty to the captives
And recovery of sight to the blind,
To set at liberty those who are oppressed;
[19]To proclaim the acceptable year of the Lord."

[20]Then He closed the book, and gave it back to the attendant and sat down. And the eyes of all who were in the synagogue were fixed on Him. [21]And He began to say to them, "Today this Scripture is fulfilled in your hearing." [22]So all bore witness to Him, and marveled at the gracious words which proceeded out of His mouth. And they said, "Is this not Joseph's son?"

[23]He said to them, "You will surely say this proverb to Me, 'Physician, heal yourself! Whatever we have heard done in Capernaum,[c] do also here in Your country.' "

[24]Then He said, "Assuredly, I say to you, no prophet is accepted in his own country. [25]But I tell you truly, many widows were in Israel in the days of Elijah, when the heaven was shut up three years and six months, and there was a great famine throughout all the land; [26]but to none of them was Elijah sent except to Zarephath, in the region of Sidon, to a woman who was a widow. [27]And many lepers were in Israel in the time of Elisha the prophet, and none of them was cleansed except Naaman the Syrian."

[28]So all those in the synagogue, when they heard these things, were filled with wrath, [29]and rose up and thrust Him out of the city; and they led Him to the brow of the hill on which their city was built, that they might throw Him down over the cliff. [30]Then passing through the midst of them, He went His way.

—Luke 4:14–30 (NKJV)

---

1. Which news headline best captures this passage?
   - "Local Man with Big Claims"
   - "Synagogue Scene Turns Violent"
   - "Preacher Narrowly Escapes Mob"
   - "Rabbi on Mission Chased to Cliff"
   - Other _______________________

2. What do you think got the Nazareth old-timers so upset with Jesus?
    - His "mission statement" made them feel guilty
    - They were spiritually blind
    - To them, he was a bragging, carpenter's son
    - He sounded like a traitor—affirming Gentiles and condemning Israel
    - Other _______________

3. Why do you think Jesus didn't perform a miracle in Nazareth?
    - The people wouldn't have believed in him anyway.
    - The crowd had no faith that he could do it.
    - It was a waste of his time.
    - Rejection of him was a rejection of God's Kingdom work.
    - Other _______________

4. Where do you find it hardest to be accepted?
    - Around strangers
    - In church
    - At work
    - With family or friends
    - Other _______________

5. What's the best way you've found to deal with rejection?
    - I don't know how to do it well
    - Stand tough
    - Try to laugh it off with humor
    - Pray for those who reject me
    - Other _______________

6. This story was just the beginning of the rejection or pressure Jesus faced during his life. Can you name areas of rejection or pressure that you're facing right now?
    - Relational
    - Emotional
    - Financial
    - Spiritual
    - Health-related
    - Job-related
    - Other _______________

7. What small step would you like to take in reducing the pressure?

OUR STORY (all) 

8. On a scale of 1 (never do it) to 10 (glad I can), how comfortable do you feel about sharing your needs and struggles with this group?

    What would make it easier?

9. How can this group support and pray for you this week?

IN BETWEEN (individual)

- What area of rejection or pressure are you asking God to help you with this week?
- Who will you reach out to bless this week?

12 THE CALLING OF THE DISCIPLES (LUKE 5:1-11)

 **GATHER** (all)

Choose one:

- What was your first paying job?

- What was the big event in your life this past week?

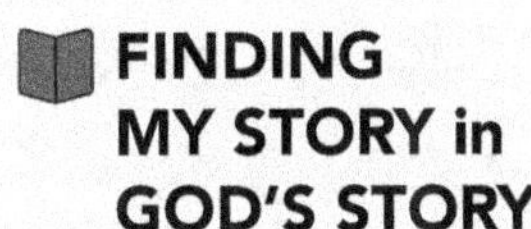 **FINDING MY STORY in GOD'S STORY**
(groups of 3–5)

Read | Discuss Questions

¹So it was, as the multitude pressed about Him to hear the word of God, that He stood by the Lake of Gennesaret, ²and saw two boats standing by the lake; but the fishermen had gone from them and were washing their nets. ³Then He got into one of the boats, which was Simon's, and asked him to put out a little from the land. And He sat down and taught the multitudes from the boat. ⁴When He had stopped speaking, He said to Simon, "Launch out into the deep and let down your nets for a catch." ⁵But Simon answered and said to Him, "Master, we have toiled all night and caught nothing; nevertheless at Your word I will let down the net." ⁶And when they had done this, they caught a great number of fish, and their net was breaking. ⁷So they signaled to their partners in the other boat to come and help them. And they came and filled both the boats, so that they began to sink. ⁸When Simon Peter saw it, he fell down at Jesus' knees, saying, "Depart from me, for I am a sinful man, O Lord!"

⁹For he and all who were with him were astonished at the catch of fish which they had taken; ¹⁰and so also were James and John, the sons of Zebedee, who were partners with Simon. And Jesus said to Simon, "Do not be afraid. From now on you will catch men." ¹¹So when they had brought their boats to land, they forsook all and followed Him.

—Luke 5:1–11 (NIV)

*Parallel accounts: Matthew 4:18-22; Mark 1:16-20.

BACK STORY*: Here we watch Jesus choose his first four **disciples**—two sets of brothers who were fishermen. To be chosen by a **rabbi** to become a disciple—a student apprentice—was a great honor. Jesus used one of their fishing boats as a teaching platform. At the close of his lessons, he directs Simon to row out to deeper waters and throw their nets in. Having fished all the previous night and caught nothing, they are amazed at the results. Jesus calls them to become fishermen of a different kind.

1. If you had been Simon Peter when Jesus told him to throw his nets into the deep water, what would you have done?
   - Wondered who this was, anyway
   - Suggested another time when the fish would be biting
   - Politely told Jesus to stick to his preaching
   - Grudgingly did what he asked
   - Happily followed his direction
   - Other _______________

2. Why do you think Peter said, "Go away from me ... I'm a sinful man"?

3. The "fishing business" was the center of these guys' lives. What part do you think Jesus plays in your "fishing business"?
   - He's interesting but slightly irrelevant.
   - He'd be a great business partner, if I could hire him.
   - If I hired him, he'd want to be the boss.
   - I think I'd like him to buy out my business.
   - Other _______________

4. Of the decisions that Peter and his friends made, which would be the hardest for you to do?
   - Who to follow
   - Where to live or work
   - What my life mission is
   - When to begin something new
   - Other _______________

5. When was the first time you felt a sensitivity toward God?
   - Don't know if I ever have
   - When I was really young
   - During a life crisis
   - Once out in nature
   - Other _______________

6. If Jesus showed up at your house and said, "Wanna be my disciple (follower) and share good news with people?" what would you want to ask him?
   - Why are you so radical?
   - Does it have to be so scary?
   - I'm ready; how soon can we leave?
   - Can we talk this over?
   - Other _______________

OUR STORY (all) 

7. What next step would you like this group to help you take in becoming or growing as a disciple of Jesus?

8. How can this group pray for you this week?

IN BETWEEN (individual)

- Set an "appointment" (someplace you can get away, alone) with God to talk about what it would mean for you to be his disciple.
- What might it mean for you to be "catching people" for Jesus this week? Serving, encouraging, sharing his love for them?

13 JESUS HEALS A PARALYTIC (MARK 2:1-12)

 GATHER (all)

What was the sickest you got as a child? Or the sickest a child of yours has ever been?

FINDING MY STORY in GOD'S STORY (groups of 3–5)

Read | Discuss Questions

[1]A few days later, when Jesus again entered Capernaum, the people heard that he had come home. [2]They gathered in such large numbers that there was no room left, not even outside the door, and he preached the word to them. [3]Some men came, bringing to him a paralyzed man, carried by four of them. [4]Since they could not get him to Jesus because of the crowd, they made an opening in the roof above Jesus by digging through it and then lowered the mat the man was lying on. [5]When Jesus saw their faith, he said to the paralyzed man, "Son, your sins are forgiven."

[6]Now some teachers of the law were sitting there, thinking to themselves, [7]"Why does this fellow talk like that? He's blaspheming! Who can forgive sins but God alone?" [8]Immediately Jesus knew in his spirit that this was what they were thinking in their hearts, and he said to them, "Why are you thinking these things? [9]Which is easier: to say to this paralyzed man, 'Your sins are forgiven,' or to say, 'Get up, take your mat and walk'? [10]But I want you to know that the Son of Man has authority on earth to forgive sins." So he said to the man, [11]"I tell you, get up, take your mat and go home." [12]He got up, took his mat and walked out in full view of them all. This amazed everyone and they praised God, saying, "We have never seen anything like this!"

—Mark 2:1–12 (NIV)

BACK STORY: Here we find Jesus in a residence in a city named Capernaum, where he had moved, earlier, from Nazareth. The crowd—inside and out—prevented four men from getting a paralyzed friend to Jesus in hopes of healing. So, they climbed up on the roof, removed part of the roof and lowered their friend through the hole! A family residence in Palestine was usually a small house with a flat roof. Beams would be laid across the side walls and the tops were covered with wood or brush to keep out the weather. Removing a section of roof as recorded here was apparently not hard to do.

---

1. What would you have done if you were the man on the mat and one of your friends suggested "dropping in on Jesus"?
   - No way, man. That's embarrassing!
   - Wow, you'd do that for me?
   - We can't do that. That breaks the building code.
   - Just don't drop me!
   - Other ___________________

2. If you were the "foreman" responsible to get the paralyzed man to Jesus, what would you have done first when you saw the crowds?
   - Thought, "This is a test to see how well I manage a project."
   - Suggested that we come back later
   - Called for helpers to tear apart the roof
   - Other

3. Why do you think the teachers of the law got so upset with Jesus?
   - He wouldn't follow the rules.
   - Who did he think he was to forgive sins?
   - Jesus was becoming more popular than them.
   - Other ___________________

4. What qualities do you see in the paralytic's friends that you value in a friend?
    - Faith
    - Ingenuity
    - Boldness
    - Determination
    - Other _______________

5. Can you remember a time when a friend jumped in to help you, like these men? What happened?

6. If you could call a group of friends to take you to Jesus today, where might you need their help?
    - Physical need
    - Spiritual need
    - Emotional need
    - Relational need

7. What encouraging insight do you get about Jesus and his Kingdom from this story?

OUR STORY (all)

8. Who do you most identify with in this story? Why?

9. After reading this story, what message do you need to hear from Jesus to help you through this week.

10. How can this group pray with you today?

IN BETWEEN (individual)

- Remember to pray for group members and the requests they had for prayer.
- How will you step out in mission to people where you live, work, or play this week? Jot down a reminder note here:

____
____
____
____
____
____

- How did your mission go? (Be ready to report in to your group at the next session.)

NOTES/COMMENTS

☕ GATHER (all)

When is the last time you went to a party or event and didn't fit in?

"My friends talked me into going to a party with them, but when we got there, they left me to go hang out with other people. I didn't really know anyone, so I wished I'd just stayed home."

Read | Discuss Questions

[27]After this, Jesus went out and saw a tax collector by the name of Levi sitting at his tax booth. "Follow me," Jesus said to him, [28]and Levi got up, left everything and followed him.

[29]Then Levi held a great banquet for Jesus at his house, and a large crowd of tax collectors and others were eating with them. [30]But the Pharisees and the teachers of the law who belonged to their sect complained to his disciples, "Why do you eat and drink with tax collectors and sinners?"

[31]Jesus answered them, "It is not the healthy who need a doctor, but the sick. [32]I have not come to call the righteous, but sinners to repentance."

[33]They said to him, "John's disciples often fast and pray, and so do the disciples of the Pharisees, but yours go on eating and drinking."

[34]Jesus answered, "Can you make the friends of the bridegroom fast while he is with them? [35]But the time will come when the bridegroom will be taken from them; in those days they will fast."

[36]He told them this parable: "No one tears a piece out of a new garment to patch an old one. Otherwise, they will have torn the new garment, and the patch from the new will not match the old. [37]And no one pours new wine into old wineskins. Otherwise, the new wine will burst the skins; the wine will run out and the wineskins will be ruined. [38]No, new wine must be poured into new wineskins. [39]And no one after drinking old wine wants the new, for they say, 'The old is better.'"

—Luke 5:27–39 (NIV)

BACK STORY*: The story refers to two groups scorned by the religious leaders and some common people—sinners and **tax collectors**. Levi, also known as **Matthew**, the next chosen to be one of Jesus' disciples, was a tax collector. He may even have been the one who collected taxes from Peter and the other disciples in their fishing business. Levi, who appears to enjoy a healthy savings account, throws a grand party to introduce Jesus to his neighbors and colleagues. This does not sit well with the legalists of the day who made it a point to avoid the sinners and tax collectors.

*Parallel accounts:
Matthew 9:9–17 and Mark 2:13–22.

FINDING MY STORY in GOD'S STORY
(groups of 3–5)

1. If you'd been standing in the crowd when Jesus called Levi to follow him, what sounds do you think you'd have heard?
   * Disgust
   * Gasps
   * Anger
   * Groans
   * Other ________________

2. What do you think was going through Jesus' mind when he chose Levi?
   * I need a good author who can write part of the Bible.
   * This will show those Pharisees who's in charge.
   * I need someone who can pay attention to detail.
   * We need to make sure that all sorts of people are on this team.
   * Other ________________

3. Why do you think Jesus attended a dinner party with a bunch of tax collectors and "sinners"?
   * It was just natural for him to hang out with "unacceptable" people.
   * To talk them into changing
   * Jesus liked parties.
   * To teach the Pharisees a lesson
   * I'm not sure—I don't think I would have gone.
   * Other ________________

4. What do you think Jesus meant
    when he said, "I have not come
    to call the righteous, but sinners
    to repentance?"
    - Jesus came to help anyone
      who wants help.
    - Arrogant "righteous" people
      don't think they need help.
    - Disenfranchised people are
      usually willing to receive
      help.
    - All of us can have hope.
    - Other __________________

5. How do you usually relate to
    people who others tend to look
    down on?
    - As Levi—party with them
    - As a Pharisee—judge them
    - As the disciples—unsure
      about them
    - As Jesus—reach out to them
    - Other __________________

6. After walking through this day
    with Jesus, what one BIG ques-
    tion would you want to ask him
    after the party?

7. On a scale of 1 (low) to 10
    (high), how receptive are you
    to "new wine" (new things;
    change)?
    - Please, don't change a thing.
    - I only want change if it's
      done slowly.
    - I'm all for change if I'm sure
      it's God's doing.
    - I'm a revolutionary—let's turn
      the world upside down!
    - Other __________________

OUR STORY (all) 

8. What starting step can you take
    this week to reach out to per-
    sons considered unacceptable?
    How can this group help you
    take it?

9. What prayer requests do you
    have for this group?

IN BETWEEN (individual)

- What step are you going to take
  this week to connect with someone
  that most people think is unacceptable?
- Remember to pray for other
  group members as they reach
  out to "unacceptable" people
  as well.

NOTES/COMMENTS

15 JESUS CALMS THE STORM (MARK 4:35-41)

 **GATHER** (all)

Choose one:

- When were you stranded by a storm or natural disaster?

- Who in your family is good at keeping calm during the storms of life? How do they do it?

 **FINDING MY STORY in GOD'S STORY** (groups of 3–5)

Read | Discuss Questions

[35] As evening came, Jesus said to his disciples, "Let's cross to the other side of the lake." [36] So they took Jesus in the boat and started out, leaving the crowds behind (although other boats followed). [37] But soon a fierce storm came up. High waves were breaking into the boat, and it began to fill with water.

[38] Jesus was sleeping at the back of the boat with his head on a cushion. The disciples woke him up, shouting, "Teacher, don't you care that we're going to drown?"

[39] When Jesus woke up, he rebuked the wind and said to the waves, "Silence! Be still!" Suddenly the wind stopped, and there was a great calm. [40] Then he asked them, "Why are you afraid? Do you still have no faith?"

[41] The disciples were absolutely terrified. "Who is this man?" they asked each other. "Even the wind and waves obey him!"

—Mark 4:35–41 (NLT)

BACK STORY*: This story unfolds after Jesus has spent the day teaching a large crowd. As they cross the **Sea of Galilee,** a violent storm erupts. Mark tells us that Jesus was in the stern—a raised section at the rear, relatively protected from the wind and water—asleep. The disciples first fear the power of the storm...and then fear the power of Jesus over the storm. They question Jesus' concern for them because he is sleeping. Jesus questions the disciples' trust in Him.

*Parallel accounts: Matthew 8:18-27; Luke 8:22–25.

1. If you were a news reporter for *The Galilee Globe*, riding in this boat, what would be your headline for tomorrow's news?
   - "All ready to jump overboard"
   - "Fishermen scream for help"
   - "Jesus sleeps through storm"
   - Other _______________

2. Why do you think the disciples decided to wake up Jesus?
   - They were afraid for his life.
   - They were afraid for their lives.
   - They needed help bailing water.
   - They wanted him to perform a miracle.
   - Other _______________

3. What tone do you hear in Jesus' voice when he asks, "Do you still have no faith"?
   - Scolding
   - Compassion
   - Disappointment
   - Frustration
   - Other _______________

4. First we hear the disciples challenge Jesus for not caring about them, then in the last statement they marvel at his power. All this after watching him perform many miracles. What do you think was going on in their minds?

5. When do you have the biggest "storms" in your life?
   - Pressure at work
   - Family problems
   - Hassles in relationships
   - Financial difficulties
   - Health problems
   - Other _______________

6. How would you compare the way you handle life's "storms" with how the disciples handled the storm?

7. How is your own life, right now, like the storm in this story?
   - Smooth sailing
   - Sensing a storm brewing
   - Sinking fast
   - Storm's over—I'm recovering
   - Other _______________

8. To what one storm or stress do you wish Jesus would say "Silence! Be still!"?

OUR STORY (all) 

9. Who in this group do you want to thank for bringing Jesus' calm to you today?

10. How can this group support you this coming week?

IN BETWEEN (individual)

- Remember to pray for one another's storms this week.
- How else can you help group members through their storms? What action do you need to take to help them?
- Do it!

16 JESUS HEALS A BLEEDING WOMAN (MARK 5:24-34)

GATHER (all)

How do you feel when you are crowded into an elevator or subway?

BACK STORY*: In this story, Jesus had just agreed to go to the home of a man whose young daughter was dying. On the way, he encounters a woman who had likely suffered from ongoing menstrual bleeding for 12 years. One can only imagine what she had endured at the hands of medical practitioners of that time. Her religious life and her ability to function in society was greatly restricted because of Jewish law. The disciples, aware of the proximity of the crowd pressing along to see what Jesus would do for the dying girl, are dumbfounded at Jesus' question. Jesus not only heals the woman but blesses her: "Go in peace."

Read | Discuss Questions

²⁴So Jesus went with him, and a great multitude followed Him and thronged Him.

²⁵Now a certain woman had a flow of blood for twelve years, ²⁶and had suffered many things from many physicians. She had spent all that she had and was no better, but rather grew worse. ²⁷When she heard about Jesus, she came behind Him in the crowd and touched His garment. ²⁸For she said, "If only I may touch His clothes, I shall be made well."

²⁹ mmediately the fountain of her blood was dried up, and she felt in her body that she was healed of the affliction. ³⁰And Jesus, immediately knowing in Himself that power had gone out of Him, turned around in the crowd and said, "Who touched My clothes?"

³¹But His disciples said to Him, "You see the multitude thronging You, and You say, 'Who touched Me?'"

³²And He looked around to see her who had done this thing. ³³But the woman, fearing and trembling, knowing what had happened to her, came and fell down before Him and told Him the whole truth. ³⁴And He said to her, "Daughter, your faith has made you well. Go in peace, and be healed of your affliction."

—Mark 5:24–34 (NKJV)

*Parallel accounts:
Matthew 9:20-22, Luke 8:43-48.

---

1. What sensations would you probably have experienced, walking in this crowd around Jesus?
   - The smell of sweat
   - Too many people, too close to my space
   - Wow, this is amazing!
   - The noise is just too loud
   - Other _______________

2. Which of this woman's problems, do you think was the greatest?
   - Physical suffering
   - Financially drained
   - Being a social outcast
   - Being religiously impure
   - Guilt and low self-esteem
   - Other _______________

3. If you were this woman, how would you have found the courage to touch Jesus' clothing?
   - Didn't have anything to lose
   - Believing I'd be healed
   - Thinking I could slip away unnoticed
   - Other _______________

4. Why do you think it was important for Jesus to know who touched him?
   - So the crowd would know a miracle had taken place
   - So he could point out the woman's great faith
   - To provide social healing with her physical healing
   - Other _______________

5. What part of this story is most significant for where you are today?
    - Jesus delayed helping a wealthy man to help a common woman.
    - The woman's faith
    - Jesus paid attention to an individual in a crowd.
    - The woman was healed by just touching Jesus' garment.
    - Other ___________________

6. How does this woman remind you of yourself?
    - Having pain that no one can heal
    - I can't identify with her
    - Feeling alone
    - Being shy about asking for help

7. Can you remember being desperate for God's help? If so, what happened?

OUR STORY (all) 

8. If you could sneak up behind Jesus, to touch him, what part of your life could use his healing?

9. How can this group help you this week, in moving toward "touching" Jesus?

IN BETWEEN (individual)

- What steps are you taking toward stretching your faith—expecting Jesus to make a difference in part of your life?
- Write a note about what you're experiencing, to share with the group at your next meeting.

NOTES/COMMENTS

17 JESUS FEEDS 5,000 (MARK 6:30-44)

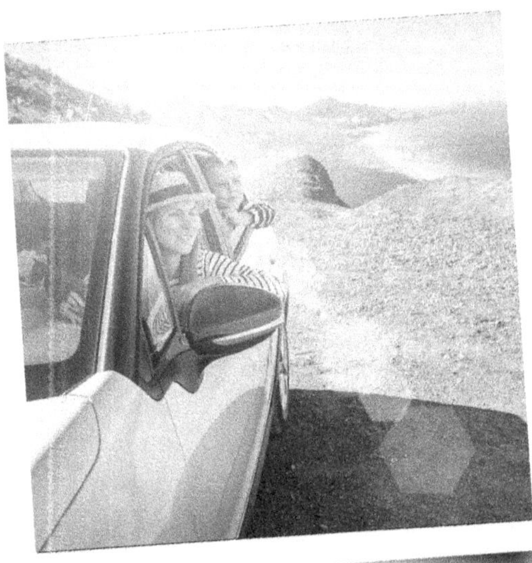

GATHER (all)

Where would you most like to go on vacation or to get a break?

"We took our kids once and drove the coast of California. I've always wanted to go back and do that again."

BACK STORY*: Jesus is attracting larger and larger crowds seeking his teaching, but perhaps more so, his healing powers. The setting for this miracle begins at the point when his disciples, in pairs of two, return from their first real-time ministry assignment. Jesus is trying to debrief their experiences but the crowd distractions are such that he seeks out a quiet site to eat, talk, and rest. Some in the crowd spot them, hurry on foot along the shore, and beat them to their retreat. Many more than 5,000 are fed with just five loaves of bread and two fish.

**Parallel accounts: Matthew 14:13–21; Luke 9:10–17.*

Read | Discuss Questions

30-31 The apostles then rendezvoused with Jesus and reported on all that they had done and taught. Jesus said, "Come off by yourselves; let's take a break and get a little rest." For there was constant coming and going. They didn't even have time to eat.
32-34 So they got in the boat and went off to a remote place by themselves. Someone saw them going and the word got around. From the surrounding towns people went out on foot, running, and got there ahead of them. When Jesus arrived, he saw this huge crowd. At the sight of them, his heart broke—like sheep with no shepherd they were. He went right to work teaching them.
35-36 When his disciples thought this had gone on long enough—it was now quite late in the day—they interrupted: "We are a long way out in the country, and it's very late. Pronounce a benediction and send these folks off so they can get some supper."

37 Jesus said, "You do it. Fix supper for them."
They replied, "Are you serious? You want us to go spend a fortune on food for their supper?"
38 But he was quite serious. "How many loaves of bread do you have? Take an inventory."
That didn't take long. "Five," they said, "plus two fish."
39-44 Jesus got them all to sit down in groups of fifty or a hundred—they looked like a patchwork quilt of wildflowers spread out on the green grass! He took the five loaves and two fish, lifted his face to heaven in prayer, blessed, broke, and gave the bread to the disciples, and the disciples in turn gave it to the people. He did the same with the fish. They all ate their fill. The disciples gathered twelve baskets of leftovers. More than five thousand were at the supper.

—Mark 6:30–44 (MSG)

---

1. As one of the disciples, what would you have expected when Jesus said, "Come off by yourselves; let's take a break and get a little rest"?
   - Ah, a quiet little vacation!
   - Time alone with Jesus.
   - Now we'll have some fun and recreation.
   - I'll take anything but people.
   - Other _______________________

2. Surprise! When you arrive at the spot, there are 5,000 men, plus women and children, waiting for you. How do you feel?
   - Delighted
   - Frustrated
   - Overwhelmed
   - Compassionate
   - Other _______________________

3. If you had been leading this group (and knowing your "leadership style") how would you have handled this situation—the crowd joining your vacation?

4. What do you think Jesus was really trying to communicate to the disciples when he said, "You do it. Fix supper for them"?
   - Show some leadership and take responsibility here.
   - Get busy checking out the resources.

- Literally, start cooking.
- Learn how to give when you don't feel like it.
- Other _______________

5. How do you like to unwind after a busy/stressful day?
    - Time alone
    - Reading the paper
    - A nice meal
    - Exercise
    - Other _______________

6. What's your typical attitude toward serving your family or friends, when you're tired?
    - Service with a smile!
    - "I think I'll turn in early."
    - "I have to fix what??"
    - "How about *you* serve *me*."
    - Other _______________

7. Where do you need to experience Jesus' compassion or his help to show compassion?
    - At home
    - At work
    - In relationships
    - Other _______________

OUR STORY (all) 

8. Jesus had compassion on the crowd, even when he was exhausted. What step do you need to take toward a more compassionate life?

- Go on a mission trip
- Provide food/clothing for the needy
- Mentor a "troubled" youth
- Serve my family
- Other _______________

9. How do you need this group's help, this week, to take your first step toward a more compassionate life?
    - Prayer
    - A text
    - A personal visit
    - Other _______________
    Each person choose one person to contact.

10. Discuss and pray about what this group could do together, to help someone in need.
    Who will take the lead to help make it happen?

IN BETWEEN (individual)

- Remember to contact your person in the way they need help to take their step toward living more compassionately.
- Begin to make specific plans, with the group, for your caring for someone in need.

18 JESUS WALKS ON WATER (MATTHEW 14:22-33)

☕ GATHER (all)

Describe your most daring adventure.

"As a child, my greatest adventure was probably hiking
to a glacier with my family. But then, as an adult,
I had a chance to travel to South Africa."

Read | Discuss Questions

²²Immediately Jesus made His disciples get into the boat and go before Him to the other side, while He sent the multitudes away. ²³And when He had sent the multitudes away, He went up on the mountain by Himself to pray. Now when evening came, He was alone there. ²⁴But the boat was now in the middle of the sea, tossed by the waves, for the wind was contrary. ²⁵Now in the fourth watch of the night Jesus went to them, walking on the sea. ²⁶And when the disciples saw Him walking on the sea, they were troubled, saying, "It is a ghost!" And they cried out for fear. ²⁷But immediately Jesus spoke to them, saying, "Be of good cheer! It is I; do not be afraid."

²⁸And Peter answered Him and said, "Lord, if it is You, command me to come to You on the water." ²⁹So He said, "Come." And when Peter had come down out of the boat, he walked on the water to go to Jesus. ³⁰But when he saw that the wind was boisterous, he was afraid; and beginning to sink he cried out, saying, "Lord, save me!" ³¹And immediately Jesus stretched out His hand and cught him, and said to him, "O you of little faith, why did you doubt?" ³²And when they got into the boat, the wind ceased. ³³Then those who were in the boat came and worshiped Him, saying, "Truly You are the Son of God."

—Matthew 14:22–33
(NKJV)

BACK STORY*: Peter is often seen as brash and outspoken. In this story he takes a risk that some see as crazy. Jesus stays behind to pray after feeding the 5,000, and sends his disciples on across the lake. A sudden storm, not uncommon on the Sea of Galilee, catches the disciples off guard—but not as much as seeing Jesus walking on the water! If we remember that a disciple's goal was to become like his rabbi and do the things his rabbi could do, Peter's action may not have been so crazy. The "fourth watch" fell between 3 and 6 A.M.

*Parallel account:
Mark 6:47–51.

1. Imagine sitting with the disciples when a figure comes walking on the water. How would you have reacted?
   - Had an anxiety attack
   - Jumped overboard
   - Thought I was having a dream
   - Have no idea what I'd do
   - Other ____________

2. If you were next to Peter when he responds as he normally does—starts talking—what would you have said?
    - "Shut up and maybe it won't notice we're here."
    - Nothing—I'd have just put my hand over Peter's mouth.
    - "Must you always talk?"
    - Other _______________

3. What do we learn about Peter from his response to Jesus?
    - He was a risk taker.
    - He was impulsive.
    - He had faith in Jesus.
    - He was a little crazy.
    - Other _______________

4. Why do you think Peter sank?
    - He lost self-confidence.
    - His focus shifted from Jesus to his circumstances.
    - His fear exceeded his faith.
    - He realized how foolish he'd been to step out of the boat.
    - Other _______________

5. If you wrote a reference letter for Peter, what would you say?
    - He means well.
    - He learns from his mistakes.
    - He's willing to risk.
    - I wish I was crazy like him.
    - Other _______________

6. In 5 words or less, describe how you respond to "stepping out of the boat" and taking risks?

7. Where might God be calling you to get out of the boat now?
    - In my job
    - In my relationships
    - I can't think of anything
    - In regard to my future plans
    - In my spiritual life
    - Other _______________

8. What might keep you in the boat or cause you to sink?
    - Fear of failure or standing alone
    - Spiritual or intellectual doubts
    - A sense of inadequacy
    - Other _______________

OUR STORY (all) 

9. How do you think your faith might be strengthened?
    - Try more risky things
    - Pray more
    - Hear more encouragement from others
    - Read the Bible more
    - Remember when God has been trustworthy in the past
    - Other _______________

10. Share statements of celebration from the past week by finishing this sentence: "When I 'stepped out of the boat,' to connect with people who are "unacceptable," I learned _______________."

IN BETWEEN (individual)

- Keep looking for opportunities to bless, encourage, or serve people who've been invisible to you.
- From #9, choose one thing to work on to help grow your faith.

19 HEALING A DEMON-POSSESSED MAN (LUKE 8:26-39)

☕ GATHER (all)

Do you see yourself more as an introvert or extrovert? Why?

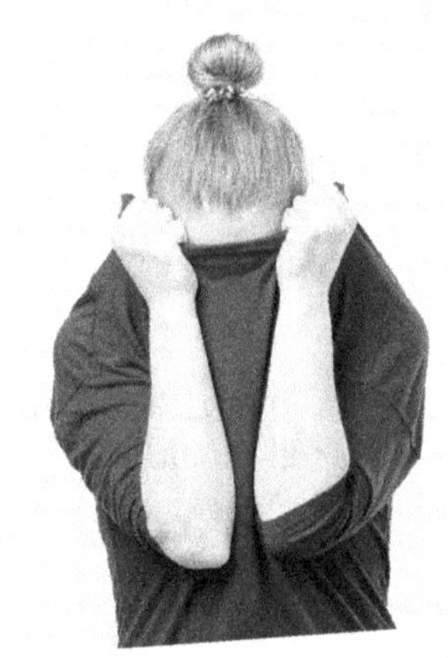

BACK STORY*: In this story Jesus encounters a violent man enslaved by **demons**. The man lived among the tombs (caves) and had been chained in an attempt to control his behavior. The fact that there were herds of pigs nearby, forbidden food for Jews, indicates that this was a mostly Gentile (non-Jewish) area. Jesus frees the man from his "spiritual captivity" and also restores his humanity. The townspeople who had feared the man, now are afraid of Jesus and ask him to leave, perhaps because of seeing their herd go wild and run into the lake. Jesus charges the man, now dressed and in his right mind, to go home and be God's witness to his Gentile neighbors.

"Definitely an introvert. I like people, and even being with people ... but sometimes I just need them to all go away!"

*Parallel accounts: Matthew 8:28–34; Mark 5:1–20.

Read | Discuss Questions

26So they arrived in the region of the Gerasenes, across the lake from Galilee. 27As Jesus was climbing out of the boat, a man who was possessed by demons came out to meet him. For a long time he had been homeless and naked, living in the tombs outside the town.
28As soon as he saw Jesus, he shrieked and fell down in front of him. Then he screamed, "Why are you interfering with me, Jesus, Son of the Most High God? Please, I beg you, don't torture me!" 29For Jesus had already commanded the evil spirit to come out of him. This spirit had often taken control of the man. Even when he was placed under guard and put in chains and shackles, he simply broke them and rushed out into the wilderness, completely under the demon's power.
30Jesus demanded, "What is your name?"
"Legion," he replied, for he was filled with many demons. 31The demons kept begging Jesus not to send them into the bottomless pit. 32There happened to be a large herd of pigs feeding on the hillside nearby, and the demons begged him to let them enter into the pigs.

So Jesus gave them permission. 33Then the demons came out of the man and entered the pigs, and the entire herd plunged down the steep hillside into the lake and drowned. 34When the herdsmen saw it, they fled to the nearby town and the surrounding countryside, spreading the news as they ran. 35People rushed out to see what had happened. A crowd soon gathered around Jesus, and they saw the man who had been freed from the demons. He was sitting at Jesus' feet, fully clothed and perfectly sane, and they were all afraid. 36Then those who had seen what happened told the others how the demon-possessed man had been healed. 37And all the people in the region of the Gerasenes begged Jesus to go away and leave them alone, for a great wave of fear swept over them.
So Jesus returned to the boat and left, crossing back to the other side of the lake. 38The man who had been freed from the demons begged to go with him. But Jesus sent him home, saying, 39"No, go back to your family, and tell them everything God has done for you." So he went all through the town proclaiming the great things Jesus had done for him.

—Luke 8:26–39 (NLT)

---

1. Re-read verse 27. If you had been climbing out of the boat with Jesus, what would you have done when this man came toward you?
   - Run for some clothing
   - Grabbed a paddle to defend myself
   - Started taking pictures of the whole scene
   - Frozen in terror
   - Other ___________________

2. Why do you think Jesus asked the "spirit" its name?

3. What most catches your attention about "Legion's" responses?
   - Their number
   - Begging not to go to the "bottomless pit"
   - Fear of Jesus
   - Other ___________________

4. Why do you imagine Jesus allowed Legion to go into the pigs?
    * He was a Jew, and Jews don't eat pork anyway.
    * Jesus was demonstrating his power over the demons.
    * So the man would know they had gone
    * Other ___________________

5. What do you think the pig farmer said as the pigs were drowned?
    * "What just happened here?"
    * "Who's paying for the pigs?"
    * "He's terrorized us for years, now our pigs are dead."
    * "Who is this Jesus?"
    * Other ___________________

6. Put yourself into the crowd that came from town. Why would you want Jesus to leave?
    * We're afraid of his power.
    * He is bad for business.
    * We want things to go back to normal.
    * Jesus shouldn't be treating this evil man with such dignity.
    * Other ___________________

7. The healed man would have been a good "model" of Jesus' ability. Why do you think Jesus sent him home instead?
    * To be restored with his family.
    * People from his home needed to hear the rest of the story about Jesus.
    * His friends wouldn't believe what happened without seeing him.
    * Other ___________________

8. Think about ONE area of your life where you need Jesus to show up on your "shore" to bring healing. What part of this story is most encouraging to you—helping you believe Jesus can actually do it?

OUR STORY (all) 

9. If you summed up the weather in your spiritual life last week, how would you describe it? Sunny and warm? Cloudy? Stormy?

    What's the forecast for the coming week?

10. How can this group best pray for you right now?

IN BETWEEN (individual)

* Focus on the area you thought about in Question #8. Write down what comes to mind. Then pray and ask Jesus to begin healing that area. Remember how he healed the man in the story.

* Pray for your group members who asked for prayer.

20 TEN HEALED OF LEPROSY (LUKE 17:11-19)

 **GATHER** (all)

Choose one:

- What is the closest that you have come to experiencing a miracle like healing?

- Who do you know that just naturally, and regularly, expresses gratitude?

BACK STORY: Due to their disfiguring disease, peole with **leprosy** were considered "unclean" and were required to live outside the camp, and shout "unclean" to warn anyone approaching them. Only after being examined by a priest could a leper be declared "clean," and reenter society. Jesus answers the men's request to be healed by telling them to go see a priest—and, while on their way, they discover they are healed. Only one returns to offer thanks to Jesus. That one is a "foreigner"—a **Samaritan**—whom Jews despised as ethnic and religious half-breeds.

FINDING MY STORY in GOD'S STORY
(groups of 3–5)

Read | Discuss Questions

[11]As Jesus continued on toward Jerusalem, he reached the border between Galilee and Samaria. [12]As he entered a village there, ten men with leprosy stood at a distance, [13]crying out, "Jesus, Master, have mercy on us!"

[14]He looked at them and said, "Go show yourselves to the priests." And as they went, they were cleansed of their leprosy.

[15]One of them, when he saw that he was healed, came back to Jesus, shouting, "Praise God!" [16]He fell to the ground at Jesus' feet, thanking him for what he had done. This man was a Samaritan.

[17]Jesus asked, "Didn't I heal ten men? Where are the other nine? [18]Has no one returned to give glory to God except this foreigner?" [19]And Jesus said to the man, "Stand up and go. Your faith has healed you."

—Luke 17:11–19 (NLT)

1. If you had been walking with Jesus when this scene happened, what would you have reported to your family when you got home?

2. Why do you think Jesus sent the lepers to the priests rather than healing them on the spot?
   - He was testing their obedience.
   - He wanted them to exercise their faith.
   - He wanted to show that healing doesn't always happen instantly.
   - Other _______________

3. If you had been Jesus, what would you have done when the one man returned praising God?
   - Thanked him for remembering
   - Told him to stop making so much noise
   - Sent him to get the other nine guys
   - Other _______________

4. What do you think was most significant about the man returning to thank Jesus?
   - As a despised Samaritan, he was the most grateful.
   - It showed that Jesus came for all people
   - He provided an example for our attitudes
   - Other _______________

5. How can you relate personally to this story?
   - Pain of a physical condition
   - Living with social barriers
   - Being more interested in what God can do for me than in God himself
   - Forgetting to thank God or others
   - Other _______________

6. What part of this story is most encouraging to you?

7. Who in your past deeply impacted who you are today? (A teacher, coach, minister, friend, rival?) What specific action do you need to take after reading this story?

OUR STORY (all) 

8. Take 30 seconds to reflect about who has served you this week.
   Who do you need to go back and thank?

9. How do you need this group pray for you today?

IN BETWEEN (individual)

Start off the week by finding a way to take the action you described in question #7. Is it calling or writing a teacher, coach, or someone else from your past?

Make a plan to do it.

21 JESUS HEALS AT THE POOL (JOHN 5:1-15)

 **GATHER** (all)

Choose one:

- When you're sick, who are you the most like: Captain Marvel, Oscar the Grouch, Rip Van Winkle?

- What was your family's favorite "cold remedy"?

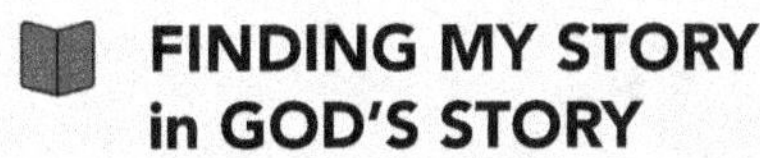 **FINDING MY STORY in GOD'S STORY**
(groups of 3–5)

BACK STORY: When Jesus returns to **Jerusalem**, he happens on a pool surrounded by people with serious physical limitations. Jesus singles out one man, asks a seemingly strange question, and then heals him. The day happens to be a **Sabbath**, and when the religious leaders see the man carrying his mat, they accuse him of breaking the law. Turns out the man didn't even know who healed him.

Read | Discuss Questions

Later, Jesus went to Jerusalem for another Jewish festival. [2]In the city near the sheep gate was a pool with five porches, and its name in Hebrew was Bethzatha. [3-4]Many sick, blind, lame, and crippled people were lying close to the pool. [5]Beside the pool was a man who had been sick for thirty-eight years. [6]When Jesus saw the man and realized that he had been crippled for a long time, he asked him, "Do you want to be healed?"

[7]The man answered, "Lord, I don't have anyone to put me in the pool when the water is stirred up. I try to get in, but someone else always gets there first."

[8]Jesus told him, "Pick up your mat and walk!" [9]Right then the man was healed. He picked up his mat and started walking around.

The day on which this happened was a Sabbath.

[10]When the Jewish leaders saw the man carrying his mat, they said to him, "This is the Sabbath! No one is allowed to carry a mat on the Sabbath."

[11]But he replied, "The man who healed me told me to pick up my mat and walk."

[12]They asked him, "Who is this man that told you to pick up your mat and walk?" [13]But he did not know who Jesus was, and Jesus had left because of the crowd.

[14]Later, Jesus met the man in the temple and told him, "You are now well. But don't sin anymore or something worse might happen to you." [15]The man left and told the leaders that Jesus was the one who had healed him.

—John 5:1–15 (CEV)

1. How would you picture the atmosphere of this story? The smells? The sounds? The people, etc.?

2. When Jesus spoke to him, after sitting beside the pool for so long, what do you think went through the man's mind?
   - Wow, someone noticed me.
   - Hey, maybe he's got money.
   - Why is he and his crowd embarrassing me like this?
   - Other _______________

3. Why do you think Jesus' question, "Do you want to be healed?" is so important?
   - The man liked having not to work to have his needs met.
   - He'd been sick for so long, he knew no other life.
   - Jesus wanted to focus the man's attention on wellness.
   - Other _______________

4. What catches your attention about what Jesus said while healing the man? (First, "pick up you mat;" then "walk;" finally "don't sin anymore.")
   - Jesus wanted the man to take action first—after sitting for 38 years.
   - Jesus knew the most important issue was the man's inner healing.
   - Walking was just part of the healing
   - Other _______________

5. How can you relate to this story?
   - I feel like I've been stuck where I am for 38 years.
   - Someone else always seems to get ahead of me.
   - I feel really powerless to change things.
   - I've finally found wholeness.
   - Other _______________

6. If Jesus dropped by your house, what do you think he'd ask?
   - "Why are you still stuck?"
   - "Do you really want to get well?"
   - "When will you quit complaining?"
   - "How satisfied are you with your life?"
   - Other _______________

7. How could you respond to his question in #6, that would help you become a more whole person?

OUR STORY (all) 

8. What have you learned in this group time that will help you grow more like Jesus this week?

9. How do you need the group to help you?

IN BETWEEN (individual)

- How are you going to apply what you learned in the group time to your life this week?
- Pray and ask God to help you grow in that area.
- Where do you need to reach out to an "invisible" person in your life? Make sure to do it, then report back to your group.

22 JESUS HEALS A MAN BORN BLIND (JOHN 9:1-34)

 **GATHER** (all)

Choose one:

- Who is someone you admire because they have overcome a disability?

- What is the best "mud adventure" (or "mud misadventure") you had as a child?

"I grew up beside a river. We loved climbing on the rocks in the shallow water beneath a bridge ... and we often came home covered in mud!"

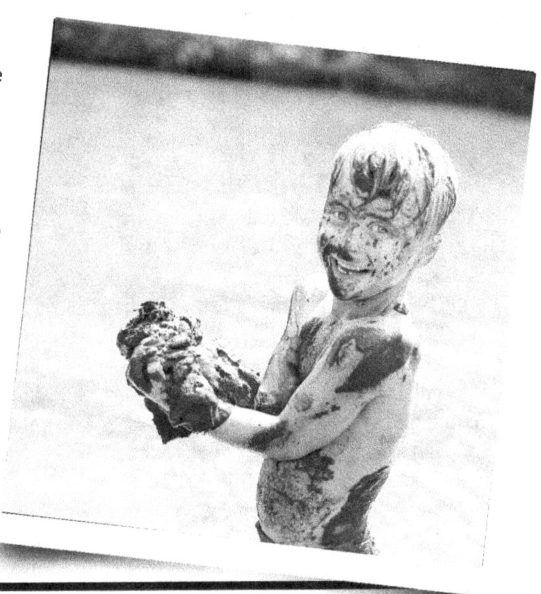

BACK STORY: When Jesus' disciples ask him why a man was born blind, they imply that disabilities are a punishment for someone's sin. Jesus dispells that idea and heals the man; but then the story gets interesting. It is a **Sabbath**—trouble enough—but in the scene that unfolds the man is accused of lying about being blind, others claim he just looks like the blind man, his parents are called to identify him, and the man is thrown out of the court. Along the way the religious leaders debate who Jesus could be.

Read | Discuss Questions

[1]As Jesus was walking along, he saw a man who had been blind from birth. [2]"Rabbi," his disciples asked him, "why was this man born blind? Was it because of his own sins or his parents' sins?"

[3]"It was not because of his sins or his parents' sins," Jesus answered. "This happened so the power of God could be seen in him." ...

[6]Then he spit on the ground, made mud with the saliva, and spread the mud over the blind man's eyes. [7]He told him, "Go wash yourself in the pool of Siloam" (Siloam means "sent"). So the man went and washed and came back seeing!

[8]His neighbors and others who knew him as a blind beggar asked each other, "Isn't this the man who used to sit and beg?" [9]Some said he was, and others said, "No, he just looks like him!"

But the beggar kept saying, "Yes, I am the same one!"

[10]They asked, "Who healed you? What happened?"

[11]He told them, "The man they call Jesus made mud and spread it over my eyes and told me, 'Go to the pool of Siloam and wash yourself.' So I went and washed, and now I can see!"...

[13]Then they took the man who had been blind to the Pharisees, [14]because it was on the Sabbath that Jesus had made the mud and healed him. [15]The Pharisees asked the man all about it. So he told them, "He put the mud over my eyes, and when I washed it away, I could see!"...

[18]The Jewish leaders still refused to believe the man had been blind and could now see, so they called in his parents. [19]They asked them, "Is this your son? Was he born blind? If so, how can he now see?"

[20]His parents replied, "We know this is our son and that he was born blind, [21]but we don't know how he can see or who healed him. Ask him. He is old enough to speak for himself."...

[24]So for the second time they called in the man who had been blind and told him, "God should get the glory for this, because we know this man Jesus is a sinner."

[25]"I don't know whether he is a sinner," the man replied. "But I know this: I was blind, and now I can see!"

[26]"But what did he do?" they asked. "How did he heal you?"

[27]"Look!" the man exclaimed. "I told you once. Didn't you listen? Why do you want to hear it again? Do you want to become his disciples, too?"

[28]Then they cursed him and said, "You are his disciple, but we are disciples of Moses! [29]We know God spoke to Moses, but we don't even know where this man comes from."

[30]"Why, that's very strange!" the man replied. "He healed my eyes, and yet you don't know where he comes from? [31]We know that God doesn't listen to sinners, but he is ready to hear those who worship him and do his will. [32]Ever since the world began, no one has been able to open the eyes of someone born blind. [33]If this man were not from God, he couldn't have done it."

[34]"You were born a total sinner!" they answered. "Are you trying to teach us?"

And they threw him out of the synagogue.

—John 9:1–34 (NLT)

1. Which part of this story would you have most liked to witness? Why?
    - Verses 1–5: The disciples' discussion with Jesus
    - Vs. 6–12: The mud healing
    - Vs. 13–17: A visit with the Pharisees
    - Vs. 18–23: A talk with the parents
    - Vs. 24–34: Visit #2 with the Pharisees
    - Other _______________

2. How would you have felt, as the blind man, when Jesus put mud on your eyes?
    - Everyone's going to laugh.
    - I hope this crazy idea works.
    - I'm ready to try anything.
    - Other _______________

3. What did Jesus' reply to the disciples show about how he viewed the man's affliction?
    - The theology of the day was misguided.
    - Suffering just happens.
    - The purpose was more important than its cause.
    - Other _______________

4. Why do you think Jesus used the mud-pack healing method?
    - Just to show he could do it
    - To provoke the Pharisees
    - To allow the man to demonstrate his faith
    - Other _______________

5. If you were a Pharisee, why do you think you'd have been so angry?
    - Jesus violated our Sabbath rules.
    - No blind man is going to make us look bad.
    - We were "blind" to who Jesus was.
    - We didn't want to believe the healing was real.
    - Other _______________

6. What is the first "sight" you would want the former blind man to see? Why that one?
    - A mountain lake
    - A sunset
    - A baby
    - Other _______________

7. The various people in this story were struggling to figure out who Jesus was. What insights have you gained about who Jesus might be?

8. What big question do you still have, that you'd like him to answer?

OUR STORY (all) 

9. On a scale of 1 (20/20) to 10 (nearly blind), how would you rate your spiritual vision (understanding who Jesus is) today?

10. What next step could help improve your spiritual vision?

11. How should this group pray for you this week?

IN BETWEEN (individual)

- What step are you going to work on this week to improve your spiritual vision? When will you start?
- Pray for other group members.

23 THE BEATITUDES (MATTHEW 5:1-12)

☕ GATHER (all)

Choose one:

- What person in your life has taught you the most about improving your attitude and character?

- Who in your family would you nominate for a Nobel Peace Prize—as the family peacemaker?

BACK STORY*:
A diverse crowd has gathered as Jesus delivers his inaugural address, announcing that the **Kingdom of Heaven** has come to earth. (Matthew 4:25.) Jesus proclaims "blessings," not more laws. Some see the first four of these statements as a recognition that God knows our condition: beaten down (poor in spirit); without joy (mourning); acknowledging we need help (meek); tired of never being good enough (hunger for righteousness). Jesus says the Kingdom of Heaven is yours; you are no longer alone in your struggles. You will be comforted. You will be satisfied. Feel like nobodies? No; you are the salt of the earth.

*Parallel account:
Luke 6:20–23

Read | Discuss Questions

¹Now when Jesus saw the crowds, he went up on a mountainside and sat down. His disciples came to him, ² and he began to teach them. He said:

³ "Blessed are the poor in spirit,
  for theirs is the kingdom of heaven.
⁴ Blessed are those who mourn,
  for they will be comforted.
⁵ Blessed are the meek,
  for they will inherit the earth.
⁶ Blessed are those who hunger and thirst for righteousness,
  for they will be filled.
  ⁷ Blessed are the merciful,
  for they will be shown mercy.
⁸ Blessed are the pure in heart,
  for they will see God.
⁹ Blessed are the peacemakers,
  for they will be called children of God.
¹⁰ Blessed are those who are persecuted because of righteousness,
  for theirs is the kingdom of heaven.
¹¹ "Blessed are you when people insult you, persecute you and falsely say all kinds of evil against you because of me. ¹² Rejoice and be glad, because great is your reward in heaven, for in the same way they persecuted the prophets who were before you."

—Matthew 5:1–12 (NIV)

1. If you were one of the people in this crowd, from all over the region, where would you grab a seat to hear Jesus teach?
   - I'd sneak into the circle of disciples, so I wouldn't miss a word.
   - I'd stay back on the edges, so I could get away.
   - I'd just try to hide among the crowd.
   - I'd stay with people of my "own kind."
   - Other ___________________

2. Why do you think Jesus chose a mountainside to give his first big teaching?
   - So everyone could hear
   - To keep his disciples closest to him
   - He always went to mountains for important times
   - It was the best place to gather a crowd
   - Other ___________________

3. Take two minutes to read through this list of "attitudes." Jesus seems to be saying this is how people who follow him will "look."

Which one or two best describe where you are today? Why did you choose that one or two?

- POOR IN SPIRIT—at the end of my rope, need God's help.
- MOURNING—feeling the pain of sin; mine and others.
- MEEK—humble enough to give up control of my life to God.
- SPIRITUALLY HUNGRY—my heart truly belongs to God.
- MERCIFUL—can walk alongside others in their pain.
- PURE IN HEART—my inside "world" (mind and heart) matches my "outside" world.
- PEACEMAKER—working to bring reconciliation between people who can't get along.
- PERSECUTED—willing to suffer and (if need be) stand alone for what is right.

4. If your best friend evaluated you, which "attitude" do you think they would give the lowest score? What story can you share to illustrate why they would score you lowest on that one?

5. If you could catch 30 minutes of one-on-one time with Jesus after this teaching, what question would you want him to help you answer?

6. After discussing these "Jesus-follower attitudes," what next step do you need to take in becoming a more mature follower of Jesus?

OUR STORY (all) 

7. Who in this group gave you the gift of their story today? How is it a gift to you?

8. How do you need someone to help you this week, so you grow more mature in "Jesus-follower attitudes"?

IN BETWEEN (individual)

- Ask Jesus to help you grow in following him better. Try making that a brief prayer every day.
- Who in the group can you help to grow more mature in following Jesus? Take a specific action to help them (an encouraging note, a brief visit, etc.).

24 JESUS TEACHES US TO PRAY (MATTHEW 6:5-15)

 **GATHER** (all)

Did you grow up in a religious home?

- If so, was it public or a personal matter?
- If not, what was your family's view on religion?

BACK STORY*: **Rabbis** often taught their students prayers. History records long prayers to gods and goddesses of the ancient world. Jesus discouraged his followers from praying the way some Gentiles (non-Jews) prayed, or with eyes on the crowd's response. He even suggested they keep prayer private. **Matthew** records Rabbi Jesus' model prayer used by his disciple (even today). The last two verses are commentary on verse 12 and address God's desire for their relationships. The ending used by most today was not in the original text of Matthew.

**Parallel account: Luke 11:1–4*

 **FINDING MY STORY in GOD'S STORY**
(groups of 3–5)

Read | Discuss Questions

⁵"And when you pray, do not be like the hypocrites, for they love to pray standing in the synagogues and on the street corners to be seen by others. Truly I tell you, they have received their reward in full. ⁶But when you pray, go into your room, close the door and pray to your Father, who is unseen. Then your Father, who sees what is done in secret, will reward you. ⁷And when you pray, do not keep on babbling like pagans, for they think they will be heard because of their many words. ⁸Do not be like them, for your Father knows what you need before you ask him. ⁹"This, then, is how you should pray:

"'Our Father in heaven,
    hallowed be your name,
¹⁰your kingdom come, your will be done, on earth as it is in heaven.
¹¹Give us today our daily bread.
¹²And forgive us our debts, as we also have forgiven our debtors.
¹³And lead us not into temptation, but deliver us from the evil one.'

¹⁴For if you forgive other people when they sin against you, your heavenly Father will also forgive you. 15 But if you do not forgive others their sins, your Father will not forgive your sins.

—Matthew 6:5–15 (NIV)

1. When you hear someone talking about prayer, what comes to your mind?
   - Why do we do this?
   - "Let's close our eyes."
   - It's time to be quiet.
   - Seems crazy to talk to the air.
   - Other _______________________

2. Jesus wanted to show the significance of praying in this story. What do you notice about his comments in verses 5–8?
   - Prayer isn't meant to be a "show and tell" time.
   - We don't have to use special words.
   - Seems like prayer could be part of ordinary life.
   - Other _______________________

3. Verses 9–13 are a model of how to pray. On a piece of paper or any text app, spend a few minutes trying to put the prayer in your own words. [Note the flow from recognizing who God is, to specific needs, to relationships, and asking for help with living.]

4. If you have prayed before, what do you usually pray about?
   - Physical help for myself
   - Help for people close to me
   - For circumstances to change
   - That I could be better at following Jesus
   - Other _______________________

5. If you've not tried praying before, what holds you back?
   - Not sure why I'd bother.
   - My prayers never get answered the right way.
   - I'm afraid I can't do it right.
   - Other _______________________

6. It's puzzling that verses 12 and 14–15 indicate that receiving forgiveness is tied to our willingness to forgive others. Why do you think it's hard for us to receive forgiveness when we're unwilling to forgive others?
   - We have the wrong attitude for accepting forgiveness.
   - If we're not willing to forgive, we're not really repentant.
   - God doesn't like unforgiving people.
   - Other _______________________

7. What's one question you'd like to ask Jesus about prayer?

OUR STORY (all) 

8. Practice praying. Go around the group and let each person read their paraphrase from question #3.

9. What did you learn about prayer in this session that is helpful for you?

IN BETWEEN (individual)

- Continue to practice praying this week by writing two other prayers. You won't need to always write prayers, but it's a good way to get started praying regularly.
- Jot down notes of how you're feeling about praying. What are you learning? What is praying teaching you about God?

25 WISE & FOOLISH BUILDERS (MATTHEW 7:24-29)

 **GATHER** (all)

Where would you build your dream house and what would it be like?

BACK STORY: Jesus wraps up his **Sermon on the Mount** with a series of short parables that illustrate two different kinds of people: the preferred ones are those who ask, believe, and receive what they need from a good God; those who choose the not-so-popular, narrow way of life; those whose lives bear good fruit; and, finally, those who build their lives on a solid footing. Jesus closes by describing two houses. They may look alike outwardly, but are built on entirely different foundations. Only one, Jesus says, is safe and will withstand the storms of life.

 **FINDING MY STORY in GOD'S STORY** (groups of 3–5)

Read | Discuss Questions

24-25 "These words I speak to you are not incidental additions to your life, homeowner improvements to your standard of living. They are foundational words, words to build a life on. If you work these words into your life, you are like a smart carpenter who built his house on solid rock. Rain poured down, the river flooded, a tornado hit—but nothing moved that house. It was fixed to the rock.

26-27 "But if you just use my words in Bible studies and don't work them into your life, you are like a stupid carpenter who built his house on the sandy beach. When a storm rolled in and the waves came up, it collapsed like a house of cards."

28-29 When Jesus concluded his address, the crowd burst into applause. They had never heard teaching like this. It was apparent that he was living everything he was saying—quite a contrast to their religion teachers! This was the best teaching they had ever heard.

—Matthew 7:24–29 (MSG)

1. Write a headline for your next blog to summarize Jesus' last story:

____

2. Who or what would you like to take a picture of, as the crowds are applauding Jesus?
   - The religious leaders he had just made look bad
   - Jesus and his disciples in a circle together
   - A selfie of my friends and me
   - The hillside crowd celebrating
   - Other _______________

3. After all that Jesus talked about, why do you think he concluded with a story about houses?

4. What do you think "the rock" represents?
   - A literal rock
   - Jesus himself
   - Following Jesus' teaching
   - Other _______________

5. What does it sound like Jesus is promising to those who live by his teaching?
   - You'll never experience storms.
   - You won't be destroyed by the storms everyone faces.
   - No more building sandcastles.
   - A new way to live by following him.
   - Other _______________

6. Where do the storms (hard times) usually come from that "hit" your life?
   - Personal failings
   - Relational conflict
   - Personal crises
   - Physical pain
   - Other _______________

7. In my hard times I usually depend on the foundation of…

- My abilities
- My resources
- Other people
- Jesus
- Other _______________

8. If you compared your spiritual foundation right now to a house, what would it be?
   - Shaky
   - Solid
   - Brand new
   - Slipping
   - Rebuilding

9. In the last year, would you describe yourself as more a "smart carpenter" or a "stupid carpenter"? Why?

OUR STORY (all) 

10. What would you like to do this week to more firmly establish your house upon "the rock"?
    - Study the Bible more
    - Spend more time praying
    - Ask God's Spirit to guide me
    - Be more obedient to Jesus' teaching
    - Other _______________

11. How can the group support you in building a stronger foundation?

IN BETWEEN (individual)

- Spend time asking God's Spirit to grow you more like Jesus and his teaching.
- Look for a neighbor or someone you pass by, to see how you can encourage them.

26 LOSING & SAVING LIFE (MATTHEW 16:13-28)

 **GATHER** (all)

If you suddenly received $10,000, how would you spend it?

BACK STORY*: Theories abounded about who Jesus *was*. Near a city noted for the worship of many gods, Jesus asks his disciples for their opinions. When they repeat what others are saying, Jesus reminds them of what he is really asking. Peter responds. Jesus then tells of the power and authority that will lie in the Church he will build. The conversation takes a somber turn as Jesus begins to lay out the "rest of the story"—events that are coming in the days ahead. When Peter says, "No way," Jesus rebukes him.

**Parallel accounts:
Mark 8:27–9:1, Luke 9:18–27*

FINDING MY STORY in GOD'S STORY (groups of 3–5)

Read | Discuss Questions

[13] When Jesus came to the region of Caesarea Philippi, he asked his disciples, "Who do people say the Son of Man is?"
[14] They replied, "Some say John the Baptist; others say Elijah; and still others, Jeremiah or one of the prophets."
[15] "But what about you?" he asked. "Who do you say I am?"
[16] Simon Peter answered, "You are the Messiah, the Son of the living God."
[17] Jesus replied, "Blessed are you, Simon son of Jonah, for this was not revealed to you by flesh and blood, but by my Father in heaven.
[18] And I tell you that you are Peter, and on this rock I will build my church, and the gates of Hades will not overcome it. [19] I will give you the keys of the kingdom of heaven; whatever you bind on earth will be bound in heaven, and whatever you loose on earth will be loosed in heaven." [20] Then he ordered his disciples not to tell anyone that he was the Messiah.
[21] From that time on Jesus began to explain to his disciples that he must go to Jerusalem and suffer many things at the hands of the elders, the chief priests and the teachers of the law, and that he must be killed and on the third day be raised to life.

[22]Peter took him aside and began to rebuke him. "Never, Lord!" he said. "This shall never happen to you!"

[23]Jesus turned and said to Peter, "Get behind me, Satan! You are a stumbling block to me; you do not have in mind the concerns of God, but merely human concerns."

[24]Then Jesus said to his disciples, "Whoever wants to be my disciple must deny themselves and take up their cross and follow me. [25]For whoever wants to save their life will lose it, but whoever loses their life for me will find it. [26]What good will it be for someone to gain the whole world, yet forfeit their soul? Or what can anyone give in exchange for their soul? [27]For the Son of Man is going to come in his Father's glory with his angels, and then he will reward each person according to what they have done.

[28]"Truly I tell you, some who are standing here will not taste death before they see the Son of Man coming in his kingdom."

—Matthew 16:13–28 (NIV)

1. If you interviewed FIVE people on the street, how do you think the majority would answer the question, "Who do you think Jesus is?"
   - Founder of a religion
   - Greatest man who ever lived
   - Son of God
   - A saint (more spiritual than real)
   - Social revolutionary
   - Spiritual philosopher
   - Teacher
   - Other ___________________

2. Why do you think Jesus was concerned about who people said he was?
   - He was concerned about what people thought of him.
   - He was just trying to get the disciples' attention.
   - He wanted to find out if they knew who he was.
   - Other ___________________

3. Which statement about Jesus do you have the hardest time believing?
   - Jesus is God's son.
   - Jesus' death had special significance.
   - Jesus was raised from the dead.
   - None of this is hard for me to believe.

4. Are you more like the Peter Jesus is blessing, or the Peter Jesus calls Satan?

   Can you give an example why?

5. What big principle do you think Jesus wants you to understand when he says, "Whoever wants to be my disciple must deny themselves and take up their cross and follow me"?
   - Following Jesus isn't easy but it's worth it.
   - Living the Jesus-life is better than gaining lots of material "stuff."

- I'm not really sure what he means about losing and gaining.
- Other _______________

6. Can you list one or two things that, for you, tend to compete with following Jesus?

____

____

7. What comes to your mind when you hear the phrase "deny yourself"?
   - Stop focusing on my problems
   - Think more about others
   - Put Jesus' desires above mine
   - Trust God to take care of me so I can focus on him
   - Other _______________

OUR STORY (all) ♥

8. What would help you to take the next step in your spiritual life?
   - Correcting some of my misconceptions of who Jesus is
   - Getting to work on the basics—prayer, Bible reading, etc.
   - Confessing my faith publicly
   - Other _______________

9. Who did you encourage this past week? Was it intentional, or did it just happen without thinking?

10. How can the group pray for you?

IN BETWEEN (individual)

- Begin to work on the "next step" you shared in #8.
- Stay alert! Watch for an "invisible person" you can bless, serve, or encourage this week.

NOTES/COMMENTS

27 A MOTHER'S REQUEST (MATTHEW 20:20-28)

GATHER (all)

Describe a situation from your childhood when a parent or guardian embarrassed you. What happened?

"Instead of going to the library to study, I went to my friend's house to hang out. My friend's mom posted a picture of us playing video games ... and mom saw it. She came to the house and got me. It was very embarrassing ... but I deserved it."

BACK STORY*: This story, told in two of the Gospels, shows that the disciples have not yet grasped the essence of life in the "kingdom" Jesus was setting in place. They, like most Jews, believed the Messiah would reestablish Israel's "glory days" (as it was under King David). Here we find John and James (Matthew's account) or their mother (Mark's account) coming to Jesus requesting high-ranking appointments in this coming kingdom. When the other disciples learn of this interaction, they are upset—perhaps because they hadn't asked first. In the end they all gain insight into issues of position, power and authority in the **Kingdom of Heaven**.

Read | Discuss Questions

[20]Then the mother of James and John, the sons of Zebedee, came to Jesus with her sons. She knelt respectfully to ask a favor.
[21]"What is your request?" he asked.
She replied, "In your Kingdom, please let my two sons sit in places of honor next to you, one on your right and the other on your left."
[22]But Jesus answered by saying to them, "You don't know what you are asking! Are you able to drink from the bitter cup of suffering I am about to drink?"
"Oh yes," they replied, "we are able!"
[23]Jesus told them, "You will indeed drink from my bitter cup. But I have no right to say who will sit on my right or my left. My Father has prepared those places for the ones he has chosen."

[24]When the ten other disciples heard what James and John had asked, they were indignant. [25]But Jesus called them together and said, "You know that the rulers in this world lord it over their people, and officials flaunt their authority over those under them. [26]But among you it will be different. Whoever wants to be a leader among you must be your servant, [27]and whoever wants to be first among you must become your slave. [28]For even the Son of Man came not to be served but to serve others and to give his life as a ransom for many."

—Matthew 20:2–28 (NLT)

*Parallel accounts: Mark 10:35–45; Luke22:24–27

---

1. Who are you most embarrassed for (or amused by) in this story?
   - The mother
   - James and John
   - Jesus
   - The other disciples

2. What discussion do you imagine took place at home before James' and John's mom came to Jesus to ask for this special favor?

3. Jesus' response in verse 22 is very serious. Why do you think James and John answered, "Oh yes, we are able" so quickly?

   - This was meant to be a joke on the other disciples.
   - They didn't understand how serious Jesus was.
   - They were totally naïve.
   - Other ______________________

4. "Indignant" is probably too gentle a word for how the other disciples felt about James and John trying to get special favors. What would you have said, as one of the disciples?

   "______________________."

5. What do you think is the most
   important point of this story?
   - Don't try to get special favors from God.
   - We are called to be servants, not to strive for power and-position.
   - As an adult, don't ask your mom to seek favors for you.
   - Serving others will have real costs with it.
   - Other _______________

6. What expectations did your
   parents/guardians have of you
   when you were young?
   - Play a musical instrument
   - Make good grades
   - Do lots of chores
   - Excel in sports
   - "Be seen and not heard"
   - Other _______________

7. How did their expectations
   change as you got older?

8. Are you living up to your
   family's expectations now?
   - Are you kidding?!
   - I'm trying.
   - I quit trying.
   - Yes.
   - I'm exceeding expectations.
   - Other _______________

9. When you have a difference with
   a family member over expectations, what do you usually do?
   - Tell them to stay out of my life
   - Say what they want to hear
   - Try to see where they are coming from
   - Try to talk it through until we agree on the expectations
   - Other _______________

OUR STORY (all) 

10. For you, what is the most
    encouraging part of reading
    this story (and listening to the
    discussion) together?

11. If you could become more of
    a servant in one area of your
    life this week, where would you
    begin?
    - With family
    - With friends
    - At work
    - At church
    - Other _______________

12. How can this group help you
    take your first step to becoming
    that servant?

IN BETWEEN (individual)

- As a reminder, post your answer
  to #11 in a prominent spot. Ask
  God to help you find ways to
  be a servant in that situation.
- Practice servanthood by looking
  for a way to serve someone you
  don't yet know, but who is near
  you every day.

SHEEP & GOATS (MATTHEW 25:31-46)

 **GATHER** (all)

Choose one:
- What item from your childhood have you kept because of its significance?

"I have a necklace that is old and rusty, but I haven't been able to throw it out. I know it was expensive and my mom didn't really have the money for it."

BACK STORY: This story (part of a longer discussion) finds Jesus teaching about the "end times" and the coming **Kingdom of Heaven** using several parables. He finishes with this one, about two different groups of people. In the process we discover who will and will not be welcomed into the new kingdom. Perhaps more importantly, we learn more about the life of service Jesus is seeking to inspire in those who follow him. Both groups end up surprised.

 **FINDING MY STORY in GOD'S STORY** (groups of 3–5)

Read | Discuss Questions

31-33"When he finally arrives, blazing in beauty and all his angels with him, the Son of Man will take his place on his glorious throne. Then all the nations will be arranged before him and he will sort the people out, much as a shepherd sorts out sheep and goats, putting sheep to his right and goats to his left.

34-36"Then the King will say to those on his right, 'Enter, you who are blessed by my Father! Take what's coming to you in this kingdom. It's been ready for you since the world's foundation. And here's why:

I was hungry and you fed me,
I was thirsty and you gave me a drink,
I was homeless and you gave me a room,
I was shivering and you gave me clothes,
I was sick and you stopped to visit,
I was in prison and you came to me.'

37-40"Then those 'sheep' are going to say, 'Master, what are you talking about? When did we ever see you hungry and feed you, thirsty and give you a drink? And when did we ever see you sick or in prison and come to you?' Then the King will say, 'I'm telling the solemn truth: Whenever you did one of these things to someone overlooked or ignored, that was me—you did it to me.'

41-43"Then he will turn to the 'goats,' the ones on his left, and say, 'Get out, worthless goats! You're good for nothing but the fires of hell. And why? Because—

I was hungry and you gave me no meal,
I was thirsty and you gave me no drink,
I was homeless and you gave me no bed,
I was shivering and you gave me no clothes,
Sick and in prison, and you never visited.'

44"Then those 'goats' are going to say, 'Master, what are you talking about? When did we ever see you hungry or thirsty or homeless or shivering or sick or in prison and didn't help?'

45 "He will answer them, 'I'm telling the solemn truth: Whenever you failed to do one of these things to someone who was being overlooked or ignored, that was me—you failed to do it to me.'

46 "Then those 'goats' will be herded to their eternal doom, but the 'sheep' to their eternal reward."

—Matthew 25:31–46 (MSG)

---

1. If you were hiding right beside the "King's throne" in this scene, how would you describe the crowd?

2. From this parable, what does it appear divides people into "sheep" and "goats"?
   - Their beliefs
   - Their actions
   - Their character
   - Their treatment of others
   - Other __________________

3. How do you think you would feel if you were placed in the group of "sheep"?
   - Surprised
   - Not sure
   - Grateful
   - Relieved
   - Other __________________

4. Who has always been there for you when you needed them? What have they done to care for you?
   - A parent or guardian
   - A grandparent
   - Close friend
   - Other

5. What kind of people do you have the most compassion for?
   - Homeless
   - Sick or disabled
   - Lonely
   - Refugees
   - Prisoners
   - I don't do compassion well
   - Other __________________

6. If Jesus came to evaluate your life today, what would he probably say about how you have "looked after" him by caring for others?
    * "You're doing great."
    * "You used to do better."
    * "You're in big trouble."
    * Other ___________________

OUR STORY (all) 

7. Who from this group, or your family, would you nominate for the following gifts of caring?

    * I was hungry, and you gave me something to eat, I was thirsty and you gave me something to drink.

    ____

    * I was a stranger and you invited me in.

    ____

    * I needed clothes and you clothed me.

    ____

    * I was sick and you looked after me.

    ____

    * I was in prison and you came to visit me.

    ____

8. What can you report to the group from trying to live as a servant this past week?

9. What could this group do to help someone in need this week?

10. What is one need you would like the group to pray about?

IN BETWEEN (individual)

How are you going to help meet someone's need this week, either alone or as a group? (Remember to make sure that it gives dignity to the person you're helping.)

Write your ideas here, so you don't forget.

29 LORD OF THE SABBATH (MARK 3:1-6)

☕ GATHER (all)

Choose one:
- Did you grow up with Sunday restrictions? Is so, what were they? Do you still follow them?
- Which of your parents' rules did you break most often?

"We didn't have many restrictions in my family, but I knew people who did. They had to do 'restful' things on Sunday, like read. They couldn't eat out or shop. And some stores were closed. (And not just Chick-fil-A!) I liked that Sunday was different, and that I didn't have to do 'work,' but I'm glad we could do other things I enjoyed."

BACK STORY*:
Back in the **synagogue** on a **Sabbath**, Jesus spots a man with a deformed hand (in Greek, literally "dried up"). He may well have been planted there by the **Pharisees** to trap Jesus. Jesus asks the other congregants a question, the answer to which may well have caught them in their own trap. No one dares to answer. Grieved over the Pharisees' cold-hearted legalism and the man's condition, Jesus heals him. The Pharisees exit to consult with the supporters of Herod about how to get rid of Jesus.

Read | Discuss Questions

¹Jesus went into the synagogue again and noticed a man with a deformed hand. ²Since it was the Sabbath, Jesus' enemies watched him closely. If he healed the man's hand, they planned to accuse him of working on the Sabbath.

³Jesus said to the man with the deformed hand, "Come and stand in front of everyone." ⁴Then he turned to his critics and asked, "Does the law permit good deeds on the Sabbath, or is it a day for doing evil? Is this a day to save life or to destroy it?" But they wouldn't answer him.

⁵He looked around at them angrily and was deeply saddened by their hard hearts. Then he said to the man, "Hold out your hand." So the man held out his hand, and it was restored! ⁶At once the Pharisees went away and met with the supporters of Herod to plot how to kill Jesus.

—Mark 3:1–6 (NLT)

*Parallel accounts:
Matthew 12:9–13;
Luke 6:6–10

1. After this scene concludes, who would you like to interview?
   - The healed man—his hand is new.
   - Jesus—he'd just "stuck it to the Pharisees."
   - A leader of the Pharisees—what's your problem, man?
   - A member of the crowd—this was quite a show.
   - Other _______________

2. If you had been this man with the "deformed hand," how would you have felt when Jesus called you to "center stage" in the synagogue?
   - Terrified (I'm an introvert)
   - Embarrassed to have others see my hand
   - Gratified that Jesus paid attention to me
   - Other _______________

3. Since Jesus knew how the Pharisees would probably respond, why do you think he healed the man on the Sabbath anyway?
   - There was no reason to wait until the next day.
   - To spite the Pharisees.
   - Because he had compassion on the man.
   - To show that people are more important than rules.
   - Other _______________

4. What probably made the Pharisees so upset with Jesus?
    - Jealousy—the crowds like Jesus best
    - Spiritual blindness—stuck in an old rut
    - Legalism—gotta keep the rules
    - Other ________________

5. What is the greatest insight you're learning about Jesus from this story?
    - He was a man with a mission.
    - He didn't come to please the religious leaders.
    - He came to restore the intent of the Jewish Law.
    - Other ________________

6. How do you like to spend a Sunday afternoon?
    - Nap
    - Watch sports
    - Yardwork/gardening
    - Family picnic
    - Other ________________

7. Do you consider Sunday your "sabbath" or do you have another day for rest (to get what some call "margin" in your life)?

OUR STORY (all)

8. God's intent for the "sabbath" was a day for our restoration—for "margin." Complete one or two of the following sentences:
    - I find physical restoration when I ________________
    ________________.

    - I find mental restoration when I ________________
    ________________.

    - I find emotional restoration when I ________________
    ________________.

    - I find spiritual restoration when I ________________
    ________________.

9. What part of your life needs this group to pray for you—for rest (or margin)?

10. What next step will you intentionally take, this week, to start getting more margin in your life?

IN BETWEEN (individual)

- When will you take your next step toward finding rest or margin?

  Write the time here:

- Schedule this step as an appointment on your calendar. Don't let yourself off the hook to do it.

30 JOHN BEHEADED (MARK 6:14-29)

 **GATHER** (all)

What's the craziest thing you've ever done to try to impress someone?

"Once when a buddy and I were watching people bungee jump, I told him I didn't think it would be that hard ... or scary. He dared me to do it, so I did. (He didn't.) He was impressed. It WAS scary ... but it was fun."

BACK STORY*: Jesus' fame reached the attention of King Herod the Tetrarch (son of the Herod who was king when Jesus was born). In response to the rumor that Jesus was actually John the Baptist raised from the dead, Mark tells of Jesus' cousin's murder. A promise to his stepdaughter, made while King Herod was drunk, had allowed her mother to request John's execution. (John had publicly denounced Herod's unlawful marriage to this woman—his brother's wife.) Herod, who had previously protected John, with his pride on the line, had him beheaded.

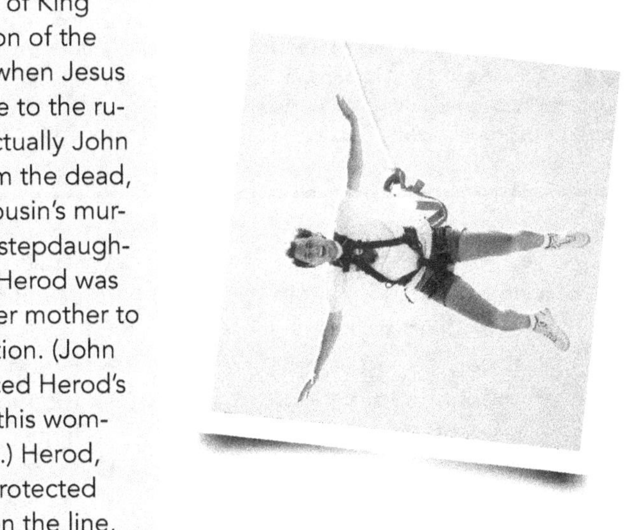

*Parallel accounts: Matthew 14:1–12; Luke 3:19–20; 9:7–9

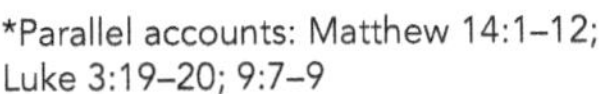

FINDING MY STORY in GOD'S STORY
(groups of 3–5)

Read | Discuss Questions

[14]King Herod heard about this, for Jesus' name had become well known. Some were saying, "John the Baptist has been raised from the dead, and that is why miraculous powers are at work in him." [15]Others said, "He is Elijah." And still others claimed, "He is a prophet, like one of the prophets of long ago." [16]But when Herod heard this, he said, "John, whom I beheaded, has been raised from the dead!"

[17]For Herod himself had given orders to have John arrested, and he had him bound and put in prison. He did this because of Herodias, his brother Philip's wife, whom he had married. [18]For John had been saying to Herod, "It is not lawful for you to have your brother's wife." [19]So Herodias nursed a grudge against John and wanted to kill him. But she was not able to, [20]because Herod feared John and protected him, knowing him to be a righteous and holy man. When Herod heard John, he was greatly puzzled; yet he liked to listen to him.

[21]Finally the opportune time came. On his birthday Herod gave a banquet for his high officials and military commanders and the leading men of Galilee. [22]When the daughter of Herodias came in and danced, she pleased Herod and his dinner guests. The king said to the girl, "Ask me for anything you want, and I'll give it to you." [23]And he promised her with an oath, "Whatever you ask I will give you, up to half my kingdom."

[24]She went out and said to her mother, "What shall I ask for?"

"The head of John the Baptist," she answered.

[25]At once the girl hurried in to the king with the request: "I want you to give me right now the head of John the Baptist on a platter."

[26]The king was greatly distressed, but because of his oaths and his dinner guests, he did not want to refuse her. [27]So he immediately sent an executioner with orders to bring John's head. The man went, beheaded John in the prison, [28]and brought back his head on a platter. He presented it to the girl, and she gave it to her mother. [29]On hearing of this, John's disciples came and took his body and laid it in a tomb.

—Mark 6:14–29 (NIV)

---

1. As you read this gruesome story of a drunken party, what is the most unsettling part for you? Why does that part stand out?
   - The booze and the food
   - A teenage dancer for these drunken men
   - Herodias's behind-the-scenes manipulations
   - Herod's weakness
   - John's murder as a reward for a dance
   - Other _______________

2. What surprises you about Herod not wanting to kill John the Baptist?
   - Herod liked John even though he felt guilty around him.
   - He feared John.
   - He recognized John as a holy man.
   - Other _______________

3. Of the people involved in John's death, who do you hold most responsible?
    - Herodias—because she set up the king.
    - Herodias's daughter—because she let her mother use her.
    - Herod—because he gave the order.
    - They're all equally guilty.
    - Other _______________

4. John dared to tell Herod it was wrong to steal his brother's wife. If you were John, what would you have done?
    - Just what he did
    - Kept my mouth shut
    - Complained to my friends
    - Written an anonymous letter to the editor
    - Said my piece and then run for the hills
    - Other _______________

5. Who do you admire most, for the way they stand up for what is right?

    ____

6. When you're facing a difficult decision, what do you do?
    - Struggle for days
    - Make a snap decision
    - Consult with others
    - Seek God's guidance
    - Other _______________

7. On a scale of 1 (don't say anything) to 10 (speak up every time), how would you rate yourself on standing up for what you think is right?

    How do your family and friends usually respond to what you say or don't say?

OUR STORY (all) 

8. This story sheds a whole lot of light on people's "dark sides." What have you found that helps you (unlike Herod) resist evil situations?
    - Reading the Bible
    - I struggle with the "dark side"
    - Praying for help
    - Having accountable friends
    - Avoiding bad situations
    - Other _______________

9. How can the group pray for you, today?

IN BETWEEN (individual)

- What situation do you need to handle better this week to avoid it becoming a bad situation?
- What steps will you take to avoid it?

    ____

    ____

    ____

- Who do you need to contact to stand with you in resisting a bad situation?

31 THE TRANSFIGURATION (MARK 9:2-13)

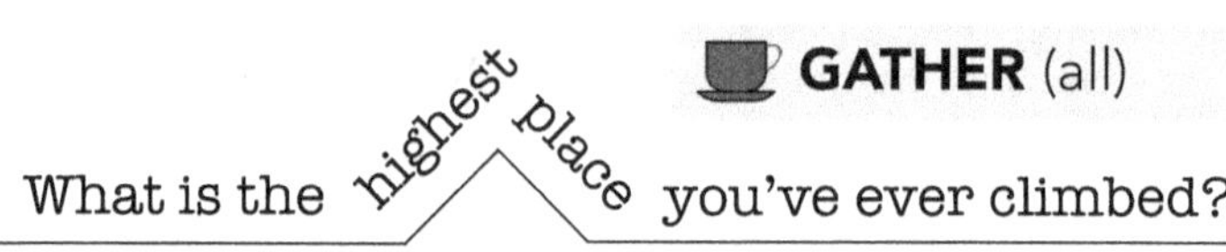

GATHER (all)

What is the highest place you've ever climbed?

Was it worth it?

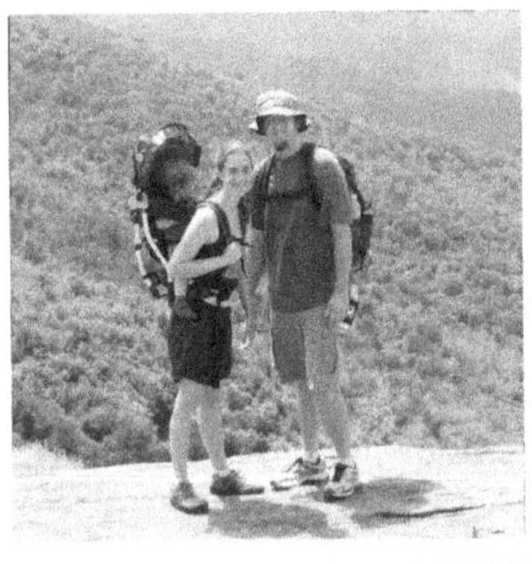

"The 'Balds' on the border of North Carolina and Tennessee. The views were definitely worth it! So were the wild blueberries along the trail."

Read | Discuss Questions

²⁻⁴Six days later, three of them did see it. Jesus took Peter, James, and John and led them up a high mountain. His appearance changed from the inside out, right before their eyes. His clothes shimmered, glistening white, whiter than any bleach could make them. Elijah, along with Moses, came into view, in deep conversation with Jesus. ⁵⁻⁶Peter interrupted, "Rabbi, this is a great moment! Let's build three memorials—one for you, one for Moses, one for Elijah." He blurted this out without thinking, stunned as they all were by what they were seeing. ⁷Just then a light-radiant cloud enveloped them, and from deep in the cloud, a voice: "This is my Son, marked by my love. Listen to him." ⁸The next minute the disciples were looking around, rubbing their eyes, seeing nothing but Jesus, only Jesus.

⁹⁻¹⁰Coming down the mountain, Jesus swore them to secrecy. "Don't tell a soul what you saw. After the Son of Man rises from the dead, you're free to talk." They puzzled over that, wondering what on earth "rising from the dead" meant. ¹¹Meanwhile they were asking, "Why do the religion scholars say that Elijah has to come first?" ¹²⁻¹³Jesus replied, "Elijah does come first and get everything ready for the coming of the Son of Man. They treated this Elijah like dirt, much like they will treat the Son of Man, who will, according to Scripture, suffer terribly and be kicked around contemptibly."

—Mark 9:2–13 (MSG)

*Parallel accounts:
Matthew 17:1–12; Luke 9:28–36

BACK STORY*: This story provides an amazing affirmation of the identity of Jesus. Peter, James, and John go with Jesus to a mountain setting, away from all the others. Upon their arrival, something happens that leaves them stumbling for adequate descriptions and for what to do. Jesus' garments take on a brilliant white appearance, and Moses and Elijah appear to them. Peter, ever the one to speak first, suggests they build three tents—in order to worship all three. Immediately a voice is heard saying: "This is my Son … Listen to him." When they look up, only Jesus remains.

1. If you had been on that mountain with Jesus, where would you have wanted to be standing? Why?

2. What is the most unusual part of the story for you?
   - Jesus' transformation
   - Peter interrupting Jesus, Moses, and Elijah
   - God speaking
   - Other

3. What do you think was going through Peter's mind when he wanted to build three memorials?

4. God declared, "This is my Son, marked by my love. Listen to him." What do you think he meant?
    *   Shut up a minute, Peter!
    *   Forget about building.
    *   The splendor you have seen is proof that Jesus is my Son.
    *   My Son has all my authority.
    *   Other _______________

5. Walking back down the mountain, how do you think the disciples debriefed about Jesus' death and resurrection?
    *   It just started thoughts in their minds.
    *   They had no idea what he was talking about.
    *   They needed more information.
    *   Other _______________

6. Try to remember a time when you were really scared. What did you do?
    *   Talked nonstop
    *   Got really quiet
    *   Cried and screamed
    *   Wet my pants
    *   Prayed for help
    *   Other _______________

7. If you were to go on a retreat, who would you take along and where would you go?

8. What might be the best way for you to begin understanding God's will for you?
    *   Be in this cell group
    *   Walk in nature
    *   Not really sure I know
    *   Be really quiet or meditate
    *   Other _______________

OUR STORY (all) 

9. How would you describe your relationship with God now?
    *   In the valley
    *   Climbing the mountain
    *   On the mountaintop
    *   Not sure
    *   Other _______________

10. What happened since the last meeting as you tried to avoid getting into a bad situation?

11. How would you like the group to pray for you now, for the week ahead?

IN BETWEEN (individual)

*   How would you like for your relationship with God to grow?
*   What step are you going to start this week, to grow that relationship?
*   Who do you know that needs your word of encouragement this week? Make sure you do it, so you can report in at the next group session.

32 THE RICH YOUNG MAN (MARK 10:17-31)

☕ GATHER (all)

If your house was **on fire**, what **three items** would you try to save?

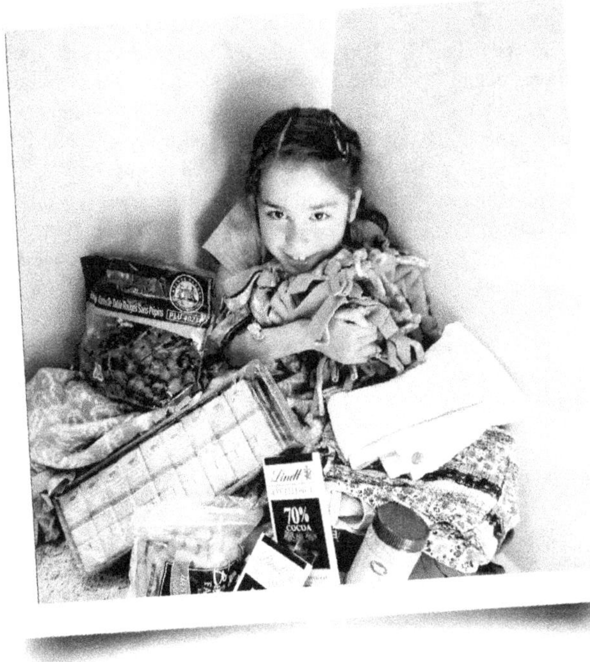

*Parallel accounts:
Matthew 19:16–30;
Luke 18:18–30

BACK STORY*: When a man asks how he can inherit eternal life, Jesus inquires as to why he used the term "good," then quotes six of the Ten Commandments. The man attests that he has kept all six, which Jesus does not dispute. Jesus tells him there is one more thing he must do, using this occasion to talk about the potential for conflict between reliance on wealth and life in the Kingdom. In the end he offers encouragment to his followers who feel they have given up much.

Read | Discuss Questions

17As Jesus was starting out on his way to Jerusalem, a man came running up to him, knelt down, and asked, "Good Teacher, what must I do to inherit eternal life?" 18"Why do you call me good?" Jesus asked. "Only God is truly good. 19But to answer your question, you know the commandments: 'You must not murder. You must not commit adultery. You must not steal. You must not testify falsely. You must not cheat anyone. Honor your father and mother.'" 20"Teacher," the man replied, "I've obeyed all these commandments since I was young." 21Looking at the man, Jesus felt genuine love for him. "There is still one thing you haven't done," he told him. "Go and sell all your possessions and give the money to the poor, and you will have treasure in heaven. Then come, follow me." 22At this the man's face fell, and he went away sad, for he had many possessions. 23Jesus looked around and said to his disciples, "How hard it is for the rich to enter the Kingdom of God!" 24This amazed them. But Jesus said again, "Dear children, it is very hard to enter the Kingdom of God. 25In fact, it is easier for a camel to go through the eye of a needle than for a rich person to enter the Kingdom of God!" 26The disciples were astounded. "Then who in the world can be saved?" they asked. 27Jesus looked at them intently and said, "Humanly speaking, it is impossible. But not with God. Everything is possible with God." 28Then Peter began to speak up. "We've given up everything to follow you," he said. 29"Yes," Jesus replied, "and I assure you that everyone who has given up house or brothers or sisters or mother or father or children or property, for my sake and for the Good News, 30will receive now in return a hundred times as many houses, brothers, sisters, mothers, children, and property— along with persecution. And in the world to come that person will have eternal life. 31But many who are the greatest now will be least important then, and those who seem least important now will be the greatest then."

—Mark 10:17–31 (NLT)

---

1. What impresses you most about how this rich man approached Jesus, a simple teacher?

2. How do you *feel* after reading this encounter between the rich young man and Jesus?
   - Sad—he thought keeping the rules was what mattered.
   - Disappointed—he walked away from God.
   - Upset—Jesus shouldn't have been so hard on him.
   - Frustrated—Do I have to give up everything, too?
   - Other ______________

3. If you were teaching a lesson from this story, what would be your main point?
   - Wealth is evil.
   - Following Jesus means sacrifice.
   - Eternal life is more important than earthly life.

- We can't work our way into God's Kingdom.
- Other ________________

4. What would you do if Jesus stopped by your house and asked you to sell everything you had—giving the proceeds to the poor?
   - Have my hearing checked
   - Compute my net worth and think about it
   - Ask if we could make a deal
   - Hold a garage sale
   - Give more to a good charity
   - Other ________________

5. How would you rate this list of life priorities today (number 1–7)?
   - _____ Keeping the good times coming
   - _____ Growing my relationship with God
   - _____ Having financial security
   - _____ Developing my spiritual gifts
   - _____ Wanting good friends
   - _____ Other ____________
   - _____ Other ____________

6. How much has Jesus and his way of life influenced your values? Why?
   - A lot
   - A little
   - Not as much as I'd like
   - Not at all

7. What would you say most holds you back from being totally open to God?

OUR STORY (all)

8. Name one thing you want to do this week so possessions don't hold you back—to embrace God's Kingdom more fully.

____

____

____

What action will you take to accomplish it?

____

____

____

9. How would you like the group to support you in your action?

IN BETWEEN (individual)

- Have you started on your action plan from #8?
- **Jot down notes** of what you're learning in the process.

- Ask God to help you keep working toward being free from your possessions.

33 A WIDOW'S OFFERING (MARK 12:41-44)

 **GATHER** (all)

Choose one:

- What is the most priceless pos-
  session in your wallet or purse?
  Why is it so special?

- Who do you admire for their
  "giving spirit?"

**FINDING MY STORY
in GOD'S STORY**
(groups of 3–5)

Read | Discuss Questions

> [41]Jesus sat down opposite the place where the
> offerings were put and watched the crowd putting their money
> into the temple treasury. Many rich people threw in large amounts.
>
> [42]But a poor widow came and put in two very small copper coins, worth
> only a few cents.
>
> [43]Calling his disciples to him, Jesus said, "Truly I tell you,
> this poor widow has put more into the treasury than all the others.
> [44]They all gave out of their wealth; but she, out of her poverty,
> put in everything—all she had to live on."
>
> Mark 12:41–44 (NLT)

*Parallel account: Luke 21:1–4

BACK STORY*: This story contrasts the offering of a poor widow with
some wealthy individuals—who sent trumpeters ahead of them to allow
everyone to see them making their offering (see Matthew 6:2)! Jesus
leaves his disciples with a lesson to consider, not only about sacrificial
giving but also about sacrificial Kingdom *living* ... and about trusting
God.

1. Why do you think Jesus was people-watching at the temple? He was:
   * Just killing time
   * Curious
   * Rating the givers
   * Setting up a teaching moment for his disciples
   * Other _______________

2. What question would you want to ask the widow as she walked away from the offering bucket?

3. If you could have given her one piece of advice, what would it be?
   * "You shouldn't have given that much."
   * "Wow, you're impressive."
   * "Thanks for being an example to me."
   * "Jesus is watching you."
   * Other _______________

4. Why do you think Jesus made such a big point about this woman with the disciples?
   * He wanted them to learn gratitude.
   * Everyone should give to God.
   * Giving is a matter of our hearts.
   * Other _______________

5. After discussing this story, what goals might you set for...
   * This week?

   ____

   ____

* The next six months?

____

____

* The next year?

____

____

OUR STORY (all)

6. What can you report about the action you tried, since the last group meeting, to make possessions less important in your life—God's Kingdom more important?

7. What areas of talent and time do you (or would you) like to donate to an important cause?

   If you're just dreaming about it, when will you start?

   ____

8. How can the group pray for you?

IN BETWEEN (individual)

* What step have you taken toward donating time to an important cause?

   ____

* Who will you serve, encourage, or bless this week? Write yourself a reminder.

34 MARY & MARTHA (LUKE 10:38-42)

GATHER (all)

What is on the top of your "to do" list when guests are coming to your home?

BACK STORY: We learn from other stories involving Mary and Martha that this village is Bethany. Mary and Martha have a brother named Lazarus, whom Jesus will raise from the dead later on. Martha, the ever-dutiful hostess, is rushing around making sure the house and food is ready for their thirteen or more special guests. Meanwhile, Mary had seated herself with the disciples and is caught up in Jesus' teachings. The response Martha gets when she complains must have caught her a bit off guard.

FINDING MY STORY in GOD'S STORY
(groups of 3–5)

Read | Discuss Questions

38 As Jesus and his disciples were on their way, he came to a village where a woman named Martha opened her home to him. 39 She had a sister called Mary, who sat at the Lord's feet listening to what he said. 40 But Martha was distracted by all the preparations that had to be made. She came to him and asked, "Lord, don't you care that my sister has left me to do the work by myself? Tell her to help me!"

41 "Martha, Martha," the Lord answered, "you are worried and upset about many things, 42 but few things are needed—or indeed only one. Mary has chosen what is better, and it will not be taken away from her."

—Luke 10:38–42 (NIV)

1. Which of the two women do you most relate to in this story?
    - Martha—responsible and stressed
    - Mary—carefree and laid-back

2. What do you think Jesus was trying to help Martha understand?
    - "Let's just have cold cuts."
    - "I'll send her to help in a minute."
    - "Sitting at Jesus' feet" is more important than anything else.
    - Other ___________________

3. If you had been Martha, how would you have responded to Jesus?
    - Gone to my room, frustrated
    - Thought, "He doesn't have to live with my sister"
    - Explained why I needed help
    - Sat down with Mary and let the food burn
    - Other ___________________

4. For these situations, would you choose Mary or Martha?
    - For a trustworthy friend, I would choose …
    - For a boss, I would choose…
    - For an employee, I would choose…
    - For my business manager, I would choose…

5. If Jesus stopped for lunch at your house, what advice might he give you?
    - "Take better care of yourself."
    - "Slow down—you're in too big a hurry."
    - "We need time together."
    - "Turn off the video screens!"
    - Other ___________________

6. What part of your life most needs better balance right now?
    - My spiritual life
    - My family life
    - My vocational life
    - My leisure life
    - Other ___________________

OUR STORY (all) 

7. What "one thing" do you think is needed to reduce some stress in your life?
    - A "Martha" to take over some of my work
    - More time for reflection
    - To learn more about Jesus and what he says is important
    - Other ___________________

8. How will you try this week to be less "worried and upset about many things"?

9. How can this group help you in prayer?

IN BETWEEN (individual)

- What steps are you beginning to take toward reducing the stress in your life?
- Who do you know that can be encouraged by you this week?

35 JESUS ANOINTED AT BETHANY (MARK 14:1-9)

GATHER (all)

Who is the "hugger" in your family?

FINDING MY STORY in GOD'S STORY (groups of 3–5)

Read | Discuss Questions

¹It was now two days before Passover and the Festival of Unleavened Bread. The leading priests and the teachers of religious law were still looking for an opportunity to capture Jesus secretly and kill him. ²"But not during the Passover celebration," they agreed, "or the people may riot."

³Meanwhile, Jesus was in Bethany at the home of Simon, a man who had previously had leprosy. While he was eating, a woman came in with a beautiful alabaster jar of expensive perfume made from essence of nard. She broke open the jar and poured the perfume over his head.

⁴Some of those at the table were indignant. "Why waste such expensive perfume?" they asked. ⁵"It could have been sold for a year's wages and the money given to the poor!" So they scolded her harshly.

⁶But Jesus replied, "Leave her alone. Why criticize her for doing such a good thing to me? ⁷You will always have the poor among you, and you can help them whenever you want to. But you will not always have me. ⁸She has done what she could and has anointed my body for burial ahead of time. ⁹I tell you the truth, wherever the Good News is preached throughout the world, this woman's deed will be remembered and discussed.—Mark 14:1–9 (NLT)

1. If your film crew reshot this scene, what would you take close-ups of?
   - The broken jar
   - Jesus' wet face and hair
   - The woman's face
   - Simon
   - The crowd
   - Other _______________

2. You're sitting across the table from Jesus during this scene. How do you feel watching a woman pour perfume on his head?
   - Embarrassed for Jesus
   - Confused; what's happening?
   - Uncomfortable
   - Amazed that she cares so much
   - Other _______________

3. Why do you think this woman interrupted the dinner at the Pharisee's house, anyway?
   - To upset Simon/ruin the party
   - Jesus had given her dignity in a culture where she was considered "property."
   - She knew Jesus would die.
   - To show her love for Jesus
   - Other _______________

4. Who can you identify with most in this story?
   - The woman—I like to show my care in extravagant ways.
   - Those who scolded her—I have a judgmental tendency.
   - Jesus—because hypocritical attitudes make me angry.
   - Other _______________

5. What are the implications of Jesus' stern response, for you?

6. What do you find hardest about showing gratitude?
   - Admitting I need to express it
   - I'm embarrassed when in front of others
   - Paying attention to times when I receive from others
   - Other _______________

7. If Jesus sent you a message that said, "Wherever the Good News is preached throughout the world, you will be remembered and discussed," how would you respond to him?

8. Complete this sentence: "This story has encouraged me because ________________

   ________________."

9. Where in your life do you need to reach out and "touch" Jesus?

   What "touch" do you need to receive from him?
   - Forgiveness
   - Strength
   - Guidance
   - Some sort of healing
   - Other ________________

10. How can this group support you this week?

IN BETWEEN (individual)

Ask Jesus to touch you where you described it in number 9. Write a note of how you see God's Spirit touching you.

36 MONEY & POSSESSIONS (LUKE 12:22-34)

 **GATHER** (all)

On a scale of 1 ("no sweat") to 10 ("total panic"), how would you rate your "worry quotient"?

 **FINDING MY STORY in GOD'S STORY**
(groups of 3–5)

Read | Discuss Questions

22-24 He continued this subject with his disciples. "Don't fuss about what's on the table at mealtimes or if the clothes in your closet are in fashion. There is far more to your inner life than the food you put in your stomach, more to your outer appearance than the clothes you hang on your body. Look at the ravens, free and unfettered, not tied down to a job description, carefree in the care of God. And you count far more.

25-28 "Has anyone by fussing before the mirror ever gotten taller by so much as an inch? If fussing can't even do that, why fuss at all? Walk into the fields and look at the wildflowers. They don't fuss with their appearance—but have you ever seen color and design quite like it? The ten best-dressed men and women in the country look shabby alongside them. If God gives such attention to the wildflowers, most of them never even seen, don't you think he'll attend to you, take pride in you, do his best for you?

29-32 "What I'm trying to do here is get you to relax, not be so preoccupied with getting so you can respond to God's giving. People who don't know God and the way he works fuss over these things, but you know both God and how he works. Steep yourself in God-reality, God-initiative, God-provisions. You'll find all your everyday human concerns will be met. Don't be afraid of missing out. You're my dearest friends! The Father wants to give you the very kingdom itself.

33-34 "Be generous. Give to the poor. Get yourselves a bank that can't go bankrupt, a bank in heaven far from bankrobbers, safe from embezzlers, a bank you can bank on. It's obvious, isn't it? The place where your treasure is, is the place you will most want to be, and end up being.

—Luke 12:22–34 (MSG)

BACK STORY*: The **Gospel** writers give a lot of attention to Jesus' teachings about money and possessions. Following a story about a rich man who died and lost everything he thought was important (verses 13–21), Jesus cautions his followers of the impact on their personal well-being—and on their relationship with God—of a lopsided attention to personal wealth. Jesus commends priorities that keep life in a healthy balance, free of unnecessary worry, focused on a trust in God's care.

*Parallel account: Matthew 6:25–34

1. Jesus takes his disciples on a "nature tour" to show how much God cares for them. If you were sitting next to Jesus and he asked you to take notes on this teaching, what would be your three BIG points?

   * ___________________

   * ___________________

   * ___________________

2. Why do you think Jesus used nature to illustrate his points with the disciples?
   * It was close by, so everyone could see.
   * The ideas were a simple way to show profound truth.
   * He created nature and wanted to show it off.
   * Other ___________________

3. Jesus is telling his disciples (and us) not to worry about the "stuff" of life. Which of the key reasons he mentions relate to where you are today? Why?
   * God will do the best for me.
   * I can relax and not stress.
   * I'll be more in line with God's priorities.
   * I can be generous to others.
   * Other ___________________

4. What part of your life do you "fuss" the most over?
   * Finances
   * Appearance
   * Having my "big" toys
   * Clothes
   * Other ___________________

5. What do you think Jesus would do if he came to your house to do a "stuff" inspection?
   * Hold a garage sale
   * Kick me out and condemn my house
   * Say, "You're doing great!"
   * Other ___________________

6. How would you like Jesus to help you be less concerned about your "stuff" and more focused on him?

OUR STORY (all) 

7. Which part of this teaching by Jesus gives you the most hope for living differently? Why?

8. As a group, discuss what Jesus might mean by his final statement, "The place where your treasure is, is the place you will most want to be, and end up being."

9. Meditate on this question: "How might you need God to help you transfer your treasure from "Wall Street" (in line with my purpose) to "Heaven's Street" (in line with God's purpose)?

IN BETWEEN (individual)

* How will you begin transferring your treasure from worry to trusting God, this week?
* Write notes on the specific steps you plan to take.

37 JESUS RAISES LAZARUS (JOHN 11:17-44)

GATHER (all)

If you could bring one historical figure back to life, WHO would it be?

Photo credit: Earl Theisen/Getty Images

"Walt Disney did such amazing, creative things. It would be great to bring him back and find out what he had in mind that he never got to do."

BACK STORY: Jesus receives word that a close friend, Lazarus, is seriously ill. Lazarus's two sisters ask Jesus to come to Bethany. When Jesus finally gets ready to go, his disciples remind him that the last time he went there, an attempt was made on his life. By the time he reaches the home, Lazarus has been dead and buried for four days. The sisters, Mary and Martha, and others are grieving such that even Jesus begins to cry. Jesus' request that the tomb be opened meets with concern, but when he calls upon Lazarus to come out, he does!

Read | Discuss Questions

[17]When Jesus arrived at Bethany, he was told that Lazarus had already been in his grave for four days. [18]Bethany was only a few miles down the road from Jerusalem, [19]and many of the people had come to console Martha and Mary in their loss. [20]When Martha got word that Jesus was coming, she went to meet him. But Mary stayed in the house. [21]Martha said to Jesus, "Lord, if only you had been here, my brother would not have died. [22]But even now I know that God will give you whatever you ask."

[23]Jesus told her, "Your brother will rise again."

[24]"Yes," Martha said, "he will rise when everyone else rises, at the last day."

[25]Jesus told her, "I am the resurrection and the life. Anyone who believes in me will live, even after dying. [26]Everyone who lives in me and believes in me will never ever die. Do you believe this, Martha?"

[27]"Yes, Lord," she told him. "I have always believed you are the Messiah, the Son of God, the one who has come into the world from God." [28]Then she returned to Mary. She called Mary aside from the mourners and told her, "The Teacher is here and wants to see you." [29]So Mary immediately went to him. [30]Jesus had stayed outside the village, at the place where Martha met him. [31]When the people who were at the house consoling Mary saw her leave so hastily, they assumed she was going to Lazarus's grave to weep. So they followed her there. [32]When Mary arrived and saw Jesus, she fell at his feet and said, "Lord, if only you had been here, my brother would not have died."

[33]When Jesus saw her weeping and saw the other people wailing with her, a deep anger welled up within him, and he was deeply troubled. [34]"Where have you put him?" he asked them.

They told him, "Lord, come and see." [35]Then Jesus wept. [36]The people who were standing nearby said, "See how much he loved him!" [37]But some said, "This man healed a blind man. Couldn't he have kept Lazarus from dying?"

[38]Jesus was still angry as he arrived at the tomb, a cave with a stone rolled across its entrance. [39]"Roll the stone aside," Jesus told them. But Martha, the dead man's sister, protested, "Lord, he has been dead for four days. The smell will be terrible."

[40]Jesus responded, "Didn't I tell you that you would see God's glory if you believe?" [41]So they rolled the stone aside. Then Jesus looked up to heaven and said, "Father, thank you for hearing me. [42]You always hear me, but I said it out loud for the sake of all these people standing here, so that they will believe you sent me." [43]Then Jesus shouted, "Lazarus, come out!" [44]And the dead man came out, his hands and feet bound in graveclothes, his face wrapped in a headcloth. Jesus told them, "Unwrap him and let him go!"

—John 11:17–44 (NLT)

---

1. If you had been mingling in the crowd around this scene, who would you have wanted to stay closest to?

2. How would you have felt if you were Mary or Martha and heard that Jesus was finally coming to town?
   - Despondent—it's too late.
   - Angry—it's about time!

118

- Comforted—he's finally here.
- Hopeful—he'll do something amazing.
- Other ______________

3. What do we learn about Jesus by watching him go to the tomb?
   - He deeply loved Mary, Martha, and Lazarus.
   - He was emotional like me.
   - He felt their suffering.
   - He was powerfully impacted by the reality of death.
   - Other ______________

4. What do you think was the primary reason that Jesus raised Lazarus back to life?

5. If you can, describe a time when you recognized that God was helping you through a difficult time.

   Who was God's "instrument" of help?
   - Caring family
   - Friends
   - A church community
   - The Bible
   - Other ______________

6. When you think about yourself dying, what most concerns you?
   - Leaving family and friends
   - Wondering what's after death
   - Hoping I'm remembered well
   - Who will inherit my possessions?
   - What building they'll name after me.

OUR STORY (all)

7. After reading this story, what message of hope can you share with the group?
   - Jesus promises that we will live beyond physical death.
   - Not sure I feel hopeful right now…still finding my way.
   - Believe Jesus when he says, "I am the resurrection and the life."
   - We can trust Jesus in whatever happens.
   - Other ______________

8. If you did it, describe the first step you took toward transferring your treasure from "Wall Street" to "heaven's street" since the last meeting.
   If you didn't, what do you plan to do this week?

9. How can the group support you in prayer this week?

IN BETWEEN (individual)

- If you didn't take your first step toward "transferring your treasure," make that the priority this week. (Look back at your notes from last session.

- Who will you serve this week?

  ____

  ____

38 ZACCHAEUS (LUKE 19:1-10)

 **GATHER** (all)

Choose one:

- What occupation would you least like to do?

- When was the last time you climbed a tree?

When was the last time you climbed a tree?

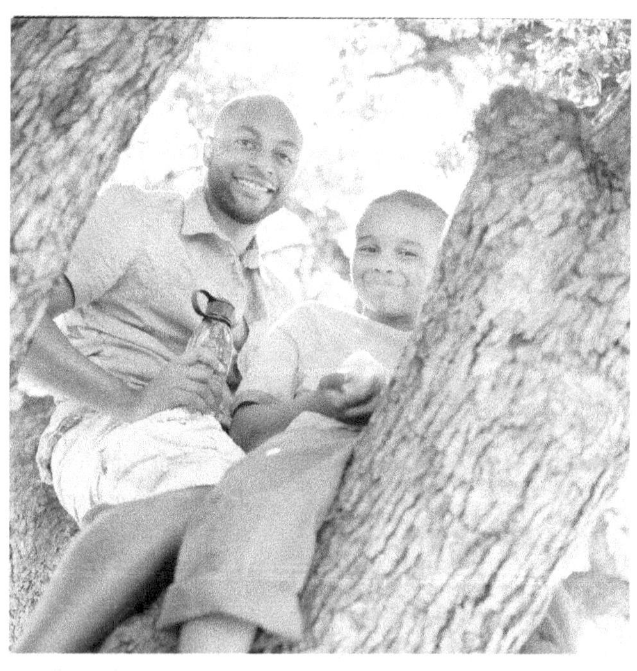

"Last weekend! It was harder than I remembered!"

Read | Discuss Questions

[1]Jesus entered Jericho and made his way through the town. [2]There was a man there named Zacchaeus. He was the chief tax collector in the region, and he had become very rich. [3]He tried to get a look at Jesus, but he was too short to see over the crowd. [4]So he ran ahead and climbed a sycamore-fig tree beside the road, for Jesus was going to pass that way.

[5]When Jesus came by, he looked up at Zacchaeus and called him by name. "Zacchaeus!" he said. "Quick, come down! I must be a guest in your home today."

[6]Zacchaeus quickly climbed down and took Jesus to his house in great excitement and joy.

[7]But the people were displeased. "He has gone to be the guest of a notorious sinner," they grumbled.

[8]Meanwhile, Zacchaeus stood before the Lord and said, "I will give half my wealth to the poor, Lord, and if I have cheated people on their taxes, I will give them back four times as much!"

[9]Jesus responded, "Salvation has come to this home today, for this man has shown himself to be a true son of Abraham. [10]For the Son of Man came to seek and save those who are lost."

—Luke 19:1–10 (NLT)

BACK STORY: Zacchaeus, as chief **tax collector**, had others working for him. He was described as rich. (Historians tell us these men, hired by Rome, made their living by collecting what Rome levied, plus an extra amount they pocketed.) Jesus spots this man sitting on a tree limb, calls him down, and invites himself over to Zacchaeus' home. Others in the crowd, who had no lost love for Jews who collected Roman taxes, are not pleased. The invitation results in a public declaration that must have left some with their mouths hanging open.

1. If you'd been hiding in the tree near Zacchaeus, with your phone, what would you have done when Jesus and the crowd stopped and looked up?
    - Tried to look like a branch
    - Called my mom
    - Taken an aerial picture of Jesus
    - Waved "Hi"
    - Other __________

2. If you'd been Zacchaeus, singled out by Jesus, how would you have felt?

121

- Afraid I'd get mobbed
- Honored that he stopped
- Excited he knew my name
- Embarrassed to have everyone watching me
- Other ___________________

3. Why do you think Jesus invited himself over to Zacchaeus's?
   - He needed a place to stay
   - To discuss his business practices
   - To give dignity to Zacchaeus for seeking more in life
   - So the crowd could see why Jesus came
   - Other ___________________

4. What probably motivated Zacchaeus to make restitution to those he had cheated?
   - He felt guilty around Jesus.
   - His heart was full of gratitude toward Jesus.
   - He wanted to be accepted by the community.
   - A miracle had happened in his life.
   - Other ___________________

5. God intended for Abraham's ancestors (the Jews) to be examples of God's love to all people. What do you think Jesus meant when he proclaimed, "Salvation has come to this home today, for this man has shown himself to be a true son of Abraham"?

6. Jesus focused on Zaccheus's positive qualities. Who affirmed you the most as a child—as a "little guy" up a tree?
   - I never really had anyone

- A parent or guardian
- A sibling/family member
- A friend
- A teacher or coach
- Other ___________________

OUR STORY (all)

7. Complete this sentence (it's okay to pass, if necessary):
   "I want to give a verbal thank-you gift to ___________________ because their story helped me today."

8. What might Jesus be calling you down out of your "tree" to do this week?
   - Stop watching Jesus from a safe distance.
   - Pay more attention to people around me, who are up their "tree."
   - Celebrate God's acceptance.
   - Make restitution for something I've done.
   - Other ___________________

9. How do you need this group to help you this coming week?

IN BETWEEN (individual)

- Who are you noticing that is up their tree, and could use your help?

   ____

- What first step will you take?

   ____

39 THE WOMAN CAUGHT IN ADULTERY (JOHN 8:1-11)

 **GATHER** (all)

Can you remember being caught "red-handed" as a child—doing something you shouldn't have?

BACK STORY:

While teaching at the Temple, the legalists drag a woman in front of Jesus who had recently been caught in an adulterous affair. Trying to trap Jesus, they quote part of a law given by Moses regarding such situations and ask him what *he* teaches. Jesus doesn't immediately answer, but instead writes something on the ground—perhaps the part of the law they left out (see Leviticus 20:10). The trap backfires when Jesus gives them an answer. The woman, who moments before expected to be stoned, finds herself alone with Jesus and forgiven.

FINDING MY STORY in GOD'S STORY
(groups of 3–5)

Read | Discuss Questions

[1-2]Jesus went across to Mount Olives, but he was soon back in the Temple again. Swarms of people came to him. He sat down and taught them. [3-6]The religion scholars and Pharisees led in a woman who had been caught in an act of adultery. They stood her in plain sight of everyone and said, "Teacher, this woman was caught red-handed in the act of adultery. Moses, in the Law, gives orders to stone such persons. What do you say?" They were trying to trap him into saying something incriminating so they could bring charges against him. [6-8]Jesus bent down and wrote with his finger in the dirt. They kept at him, badgering him. He straightened up and said, "The sinless one among you, go first: Throw the stone." Bending down again, he wrote some more in the dirt. [9-10]Hearing that, they walked away, one after another, beginning with the oldest. The woman was left alone. Jesus stood up and spoke to her. "Woman, where are they? Does no one condemn you?" [11]"No one, Master."

"Neither do I," said Jesus. "Go on your way. From now on, don't sin."

—John 8:1–11 (MSG)

1. After reading this story, what is the biggest question you have?
   - Was she really adulterous or just charged by these evil men?
   - Where was the man she was supposedly "involved" with?
   - How did Jesus remain so calm?
   - What was Jesus writing in the dirt?
   - Other _______________

2. Why do you think Jesus took time to write a note on the ground?
   - To cool off
   - To divert attention from the woman
   - To think up a good response
   - To write a note for the accusers to see
   - Other _______________

3. If you had been Jesus, what would you have written on the ground?

4. What do you think Jesus meant when he said, "The sinless one among you, go first: Throw the stone"?
   - Deal with your own sin first
   - It's your sin that you see in others
   - You're condemning the wrong person
   - Other _______________

5. Imagine the sound as, one by one, the accusers dropped their rocks. Why do you imagine the oldest ones left first?
   - They had a lifetime of sins.
   - The younger ones were too arrogant to admit they'd sinned.
   - The rocks were getting heavy for old muscles.
   - Other _______________

6. How are Jesus' final words good news to the woman?
   - Acquittal: "The charges have been dropped."
   - Encouragement: "You're a beautiful person and you can live differently."
   - Challenge: "The evidence of forgiveness is a changed life."
   - Other _______________

7. Can you remember a time when (like this woman) you felt "tried and convicted" by the crowd?
   - When I didn't make the team.
   - I don't remember a time.
   - When I didn't feel good enough to belong.
   - When I was falsely accused of _______________.
   - When people found out I was trying to follow Jesus.
   - Other _______________

8. What about times you blow it
    and convict yourself? What do
    you do?
    - Confess it to God and move on
    - Shrug it off
    - Tell a close friend
    - Try to make up for it
    - Other _______________________

OUR STORY (all) 

9. How might this study be good
    news to you today?
    - It's helped me understanding
      that I'm a person of worth.
    - I'm not sure how to answer
      that.
    - It's helped me realize how
      much Jesus loves me.
    - I'm discovering acceptance
      by this group

10. Can you briefly share how you
    helped someone come down
    "out of their tree" this past
    week?

11. How can this group pray for
    you?

IN BETWEEN (individual)

- What "invisible" person are you
  going to seek out to intentionally listen to this week?

  ____

- Write down some notes about
  what you **learn from them**.

<table>
<tr><td>1.</td></tr>
<tr><td>2.</td></tr>
<tr><td>3.</td></tr>
<tr><td>4.</td></tr>
<tr><td>5.</td></tr>
</table>

- How were you blessed by
  listening instead of trying to
  help?
  Write 3 examples:

<table>
<tr><td>1.</td></tr>
<tr><td>2.</td></tr>
<tr><td>3.</td></tr>
</table>

40 WORKERS IN THE VINEYARD (MATTHEW 20:1-16)

 **GATHER** (all)

Choose one:
- As a child, what chores did you have to perform? Did you get an allowance for it? If so, how much?

- Who do you believe works harder: the mother of a preschooler, a criminal attorney, a door-to-door salesperson, a minister, or someone else?

As a child, what chores did you have to perform? How much allowance did you get for it?

"I remember having to unload the dishwasher and put things away. And sometimes I'd get to help wash the car. I didn't get paid anything until I was around 10."

FINDING MY STORY in GOD'S STORY
(groups of 3–5)

Read | Discuss Questions

[1]"For the Kingdom of Heaven is like the landowner who went out early one morning to hire workers for his vineyard. [2]He agreed to pay the normal daily wage[a] and sent them out to work.

[3]"At nine o'clock in the morning he was passing through the marketplace and saw some people standing around doing nothing. [4]So he hired them, telling them he would pay them whatever was right at the end of the day. [5]So they went to work in the vineyard. At noon and again at three o'clock he did the same thing.

[6]"At five o'clock that afternoon he was in town again and saw some more people standing around. He asked them, 'Why haven't you been working today?'

[7]"They replied, 'Because no one hired us.'

"The landowner told them, 'Then go out and join the others in my vineyard.'

[8]"That evening he told the foreman to call the workers in and pay them, beginning with the last workers first. [9]When those hired at five o'clock were paid, each received a full day's wage. [10]When those hired first came to get their pay, they assumed they would receive more. But they, too, were paid a day's wage. [11]When they received their pay, they protested to the owner, [12]'Those people worked only one hour, and yet you've paid them just as much as you paid us who worked all day in the scorching heat.'

[13]"He answered one of them, 'Friend, I haven't been unfair! Didn't you agree to work all day for the usual wage? [14]Take your money and go. I wanted to pay this last worker the same as you. [15]Is it against the law for me to do what I want with my money? Should you be jealous because I am kind to others?'

[16]"So those who are last now will be first then, and those who are first will be last."

—Matthew 20:1–16 (NLT)

BACK STORY:
This parable begins at grape-harvest time with the vineyard owner hiring a group of day laborers. Three hours later he hires another group, and then the pattern is repeated every few hours until an hour before the work day has ended. When the workers come to be paid, they all receive the same, normal wage for one day's work—a denarius. Those who have worked a full day are not happy. Jesus uses this story to teach his disciples something about the **Kingdom of Heaven.**

1. If you had been one of the first workers hired, how would you have responded to the landowner?
   - Just like the story; complained really loudly
   - Started a workers' union
   - Never worked for him again
   - Been happy for the last people hired
   - Other _______________________

2. From a business consultant's viewpoint, how would you advise the landowner?
    - "Don't ever do that again."
    - "It's a good idea to help out those hired last."
    - "Go to business school!"
    - "Do what you want with your money."
    - Other ________________________

3. If Jesus told this story to help us understand more about God's Kingdom ways, what does this tell you about God?
    - God's ways don't fit how I was taught business.
    - God can bless anyone he wants.
    - We don't earn God's love by the amount of work we do.
    - I'm still not sure.
    - Other ________________________

4. What do you consider the biggest challenge in your work?
    - Always too much to do
    - Balancing work with family
    - Finding fulfillment
    - Job security
    - Nothing, it's really good
    - Other ________________________

5. If you were (are) the boss, and had unlimited resources, what's the first thing you would change in your work environment?

    ____

6. What attitude change might help the way you feel about work?
    - Stop looking at work only in terms of money
    - I don't think anything is wrong with my attitude
    - See what I can contribute rather than what I can receive
    - Look for ways God can use me to serve others
    - Other ________________________

OUR STORY (all) 

7. Using this parable as a guide, think about your enthusiasm level and attitude about life. What "time" is it right now?
    - 6 AM—I'm raring to go.
    - 9 AM—I'm feeling productive.
    - Noon—I'm ready for a break.
    - 5 PM—Help! I'm out of gas!
    - 6 PM—I'm feeling satisfied with what I've accomplished.

8. Who was the "invisible" person you listened to this week? What "gift" did they bless you with? (Look back at your notes.)

9. How can this group support you in your work setting this week?

IN BETWEEN (individual)

- Who needs you to serve or encourage them at your work this week?

    ____

- What action will you take? Jot a few notes to describe what happens.

41 INVESTMENT (MATTHEW 25:14-30)

 **GATHER** (all)

Choose one:

- Would your best friend or spouse describe you as more a "saver" or a "spender"? Give an example.

- Who was one of the most talented people in your high school? What happened to them?

"I'm sure the answer would be 'saver.' I'm always asking, 'Do I need that or do I just want that?' But, the last time we had an unexpected house expense, we were prepared."

Would your best friend or spouse describe you as more a "saver" or a "spender"?

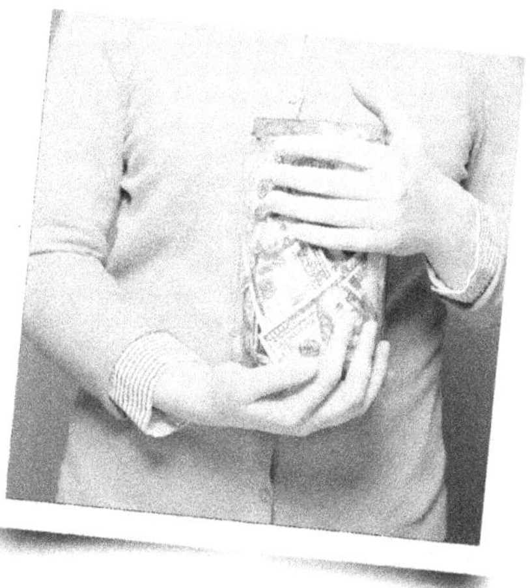

 **FINDING MY STORY in GOD'S STORY** (groups of 3–5)

Read | Discuss Questions

[14-18] "It's also like a man going off on an extended trip. He called his servants together and delegated responsibilities. To one he gave five thousand dollars, to another two thousand, to a third one thousand, depending on their abilities. Then he left. Right off, the first servant went to work and doubled his master's investment. The second did the same. But the man with the single thousand dug a hole and carefully buried his master's money.

[19-21] "After a long absence, the master of those three servants came back and settled up with them. The one given five thousand dollars showed him how

he had doubled his investment. His master commended him: 'Good work! You did your job well. From now on be my partner.'

22-23 "The servant with the two thousand showed how he also had doubled his master's investment. His master commended him: 'Good work! You did your job well. From now on be my partner.'

24-25 "The servant given one thousand said, 'Master, I know you have high standards and hate careless ways, that you demand the best and make no allowances for error. I was afraid I might disappoint you, so I found a good hiding place and secured your money. Here it is, safe and sound down to the last cent.'

26-27 "The master was furious. 'That's a terrible way to live! It's criminal to live cautiously like that! If you knew I was after the best, why did you do less than the least? The least you could have done would have been to invest the sum with the bankers, where at least I would have gotten a little interest.

28-30 "'Take the thousand and give it to the one who risked the most. And get rid of this "play-it-safe" who won't go out on a limb. Throw him out into utter darkness.'"

—Matthew 25:14–30 (MSG)

*Parallel account: Luke 19:12–26

BACK STORY*: Jesus is still answering his disciples' questions about the "end times" (Matthew 24:3) and explaining what signs might be seen along the way. Jesus spends most of his time relaying stories to spark reflection on their conduct and focus while they wait. In this story, Jesus tells of a landowner/businessman who takes a trip and leaves his trusted servants in charge of differing amounts of his business according to their gifts and abilities—and what took place when the man returned some years later.

1. What emotions did you feel while reading this story?
   - Frustrated—each servant did their best
   - Intrigued—I wish I could invest like that
   - Confused—I don't know what this has to do with me
   - Satisfied—the servants got what they deserved
   - Other ______________________

2. Do you know why you felt that way?
   - I've had a similar experience.
   - I like the way the "master" thinks.
   - I don't like the poorer man losing the money.
   - Business and finances are not my "thing."
   - Other ______________________

3. Which of the three servants do you most identify with?
   - The one with $5,000—I've been really blessed.
   - The one with $2,000—I've done okay with what I've got.
   - The one with $1,000—I always get the short end.

4. Why do you think the master was so hard on the servant who hid his money?
   - He refused to take a risk.
   - He didn't use the gift he'd been given.
   - He missed a great opportunity.
   - Other _______________

5. If you were going to write a book title for this story, what would it be?

   ____

   ____

6. How do you tend to respond when you're given big responsibility?
   - Grab it and go—a chance to use my gifts/abilities
   - Nervous—don't want to screw it up
   - Proud—glad they trust me
   - Overwhelmed—can't handle it
   - Hide—hope I don't get called out
   - Other _______________

7. After discussing this story, what do you think God's expectations are for how we invest our lives in God's Kingdom purposes?

- We need to serve with the gifts God's given us.
- He wants us to take a risk.
- He's pleased if we're doing our best.
- Sometimes he expects more than we can give.
- Other _______________

OUR STORY (all) 

8. If Jesus called you to his office for a "gift-investment report," what do you think he'd tell you?
   - You aren't using the gifts I've given you.
   - Well, you're serving at about 50%.
   - It appears that life is a struggle for you right now.
   - Wow, you're doing great!
   - Other _______________

9. As you think about the week ahead, where might you do better at investing your life (using your gifts and abilities) in God's Kingdom purposes?

10. How do you need this group to pray for you?

IN BETWEEN (individual)

- What specific step do you want to start—to better improve your life's investment in God's Kingdom purposes?
- Ask Jesus to give you the wisdom and strength, you need.
- **Write down** the action you take this week.

42 THE GOOD SAMARITAN (LUKE 10:25-37)

BACK STORY: In this scripture, Jesus is talking to an expert in the **Law of Moses**. In answer to the lawyer's query about how to gain eternal life, Jesus asks what the Law says. Jesus commends the man's response and tells him to do what it says. Perhaps wanting to justify himself, the lawyer presses on. (Specifically, asking Jesus to define "neighbor.") The lawyer might have wished he hadn't asked. Jesus tells a story about a Samaritan who cared for a robbed/injured man who considered him an outcast. The Priest and Levite failed to care for one of their own.

GATHER (all)

When was the last time someone came to your "rescue"?

How did they help?

FINDING MY STORY in GOD'S STORY (groups of 3–5)

[25]On one occasion an expert in the law stood up to test Jesus. "Teacher," he asked, "what must I do to inherit eternal life?"
[26]"What is written in the Law?" he replied. "How do you read it?"
[27]He answered, "'Love the Lord your God with all your heart and with all your soul and with all your strength and with all your mind'; and, 'Love your neighbor as yourself.'"
[28]"You have answered correctly," Jesus replied. "Do this and you will live."
[29]But he wanted to justify himself, so he asked Jesus, "And who is my neighbor?"
[30]In reply Jesus said: "A man was going down from Jerusalem to Jericho, when he was attacked by robbers. They stripped him of his clothes, beat him and went away, leaving him half dead. [31]A priest happened to be going down the same road, and when he saw the man, he passed by on the other side. [32]So too, a Levite, when he came to the place and saw him, passed by on the other side. [33]But a Samaritan, as he traveled, came where the man was; and when he saw him, he took pity on him. [34]He went to him and bandaged his wounds, pouring on oil and wine. Then he put the man on his own donkey, brought him to an inn and took care of him. [35]The next day he took out two denarii[c] and gave them to the innkeeper. 'Look after him,' he said, 'and when I return, I will reimburse you for any extra expense you may have.'
[36]"Which of these three do you think was a neighbor to the man who fell into the hands of robbers?"
[37]The expert in the law replied, "The one who had mercy on him."
Jesus told him, "Go and do likewise."
—Luke 10:25–37 (NIV)

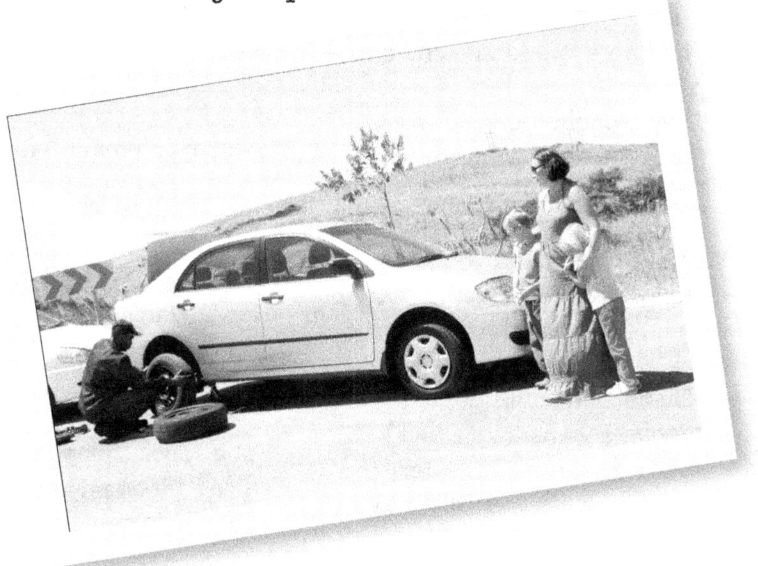

"I had a flat tire while traveling with my kids. A guy driving by saw me beside the road. He stopped and changed my tire. I was so grateful!"

1. Why do you think Jesus chose to tell this story in response to the lawyer's question?
   - He didn't understand what the lawyer was asking.
   - To use a lawyer's "case study" model of answering
   - To show how "good" people often don't do what's right
   - Because the question really was, "To whom must I be a neighbor?"
   - Other _______________

2. Which one of the travelers do you most identify with?
   - The injured man—it's been that kind of day
   - The priest—too much "church work" to do
   - The Levite—don't want my clothes soiled
   - The Samaritan—whatever it takes, I'm here

3. Why do you think the two reli-
   gious leaders didn't stop?
   - They feared for their own
     safety.
   - They were late for the church
     picnic.
   - They thought the man was al-
     ready dead—so why bother.
   - Other ______________________

4. What question would you have
   wanted to ask the Samaritan
   when he arrived at the inn with
   the injured man?
   - "Do you know this guy?"
   - "You're a Samaritan. Don't
     you know this man is a Jew?"
   - "How long are you willing to
     support this guy's care?"
   - "Where did you learn to care
     for strangers like this?"
   - Other ______________________

5. If you were on your way to an
   important appointment and saw
   someone who looked in trou-
   ble, what would you do?
   - Find someone to check it out
   - Pass on by
   - Stop and try to help
   - Call 9-1-1
   - Other ______________________

6. How do you usually react when
   someone on the street asks you
   for a handout? Why?
   - Look away
   - Give them my name, and ask
     for theirs
   - Give money—no questions
     asked
   - Offer to get them a meal
   - Other ______________________

7. Finish this sentence: "After
   reading this parable, I've
   decided that my "neighbor"
   is _____________________________
   and I'm committing to

   ____

   _____________________________."

8. How can this group reach out
   and help someone like the
   Good Samaritan did?

   Set a specific plan that pre-
   serves the dignity of the person
   you're helping.

9. How should this group pray for
   one another? One or two pray
   out loud—leader close.

IN BETWEEN (individual)

- How are you going to follow up
  with your commitment in #7?

- **Write brief notes** below of
  what happens when you follow
  through on your commitment.

43 THE PRODIGAL SON (LUKE 15:11-32)

☕ GATHER (all)

If your family threw a party for you, what kind of centerpiece would you want on the food table?

📖 FINDING MY STORY in GOD'S STORY (groups of 3–5)

Read | Discuss Questions

[11]To illustrate the point further, Jesus told them this story: "A man had two sons. [12]The younger son told his father, 'I want my share of your estate now before you die.' So his father agreed to divide his wealth between his sons.

[13]"A few days later this younger son packed all his belongings and moved to a distant land, and there he wasted all his money in wild living. [14]About the time his money ran out, a great famine swept over the land, and he began to starve. [15]He persuaded a local farmer to hire him, and the man sent him into his fields to feed the pigs. [16]The young man became so hungry that even the pods he was feeding the pigs looked good to him. But no one gave him anything.

[17]"When he finally came to his senses, he said to himself, 'At home even the hired servants have food enough to spare, and here I am dying of hunger! [18]I will go home to my father and say, "Father, I have sinned against both heaven and you, [19]and I am no longer worthy of being called your son. Please take me on as a hired servant."'

[20]"So he returned home to his father. And while he was still a long way off, his father saw him coming. Filled with love and compassion, he ran to his son, embraced him, and kissed him. [21]His son said to him, 'Father, I have sinned against both heaven and you, and I am no longer worthy of being called your son.'

[22]"But his father said to the servants, 'Quick! Bring the finest robe in the house and put it on him. Get a ring for his finger and sandals for his feet. [23]And kill the calf we have been fattening. We must celebrate with a feast, [24]for this son of mine was dead and has now returned to life. He was lost, but now he is found.' So the party began.

[25]"Meanwhile, the older son was in the fields working. When he returned home, he heard music and dancing in the house, [26]and he asked one of the servants what was going on. [27]'Your brother is back,' he was told, 'and your father has killed the fattened calf. We are celebrating because of his safe return.'

[28]"The older brother was angry and wouldn't go in. His father came out and begged him, [29]but he replied, 'All these years I've slaved for you and never once refused to do a single thing you told me to. And in all that time you never gave me even one young goat for a feast with my friends. [30]Yet when this son of yours comes back after squandering your money on prostitutes, you celebrate by killing the fattened calf!'

[31]"His father said to him, 'Look, dear son, you have always stayed by me, and everything I have is yours. [32]We had to celebrate this happy day. For your brother was dead and has come back to life! He was lost, but now he is found!'"

—Luke 15:11–32 (NLT)

If your family threw a PARTY for you, what kind of centerpiece would you want on the food table?

The centerpiece should reflect me; and how well my family knew me. Nothing extravagant. Something simple yet true to our relationship. It needs to remind me that there's a level of intimacy and connection between me and those throwing the party. That would make me smile.

BACK STORY: This study looks at the last in a series of "lost and found" stories—seemingly in response to accusations about Jesus' relationship with outcasts and sinners (15:1–2). We encounter three surprising responses as the story unfolds: (1) the father's approval of the younger son's request; (2) the father's response when the son returns; and (3) the older brother's response. In this culture, for a son to ask for his inheritance was the same as saying he wished his father dead.

1. Put yourself in the place of the younger son. What do you feel when first seeing your father?
   - Terrified—he's going to kill me.
   - Relieved—he's still looking for me.
   - Other ___________________

2. As the father, what would you say when your son got close enough to hear?
   - "Good to see you—you're grounded for life."
   - "Go see your mom!"
   - "Welcome home; I love you!"
   - Other ___________________

3. If you could interview anyone in this story, who would it be? Why?

4. How do you relate to the experiences of the younger son?
   - I've had my share of "wild living."
   - I've never really known anything like this.
   - I've experienced being forgiven.
   - Other ___________________

5. Suppose Jesus wanted us to see the father as an example of God. What might this story make you think?

- Wish I'd had a dad like that
- Can't believe he forgave his son
- My father was just like this one.
- Other ___________________

6. If you described your relationship to God as a "spiritual" journey, where are you right now? Give an example.
   - Headed back to God
   - Not sure
   - In the distant country
   - Working the home fields
   - Other ___________________

OUR STORY (all) 

7. What is the next, best step for you in your "spiritual" journey?

8. How should this group pray for you this week?

IN BETWEEN (individual)

- On a card, write down the next step you decided on in #7 and post it where you can see it each day.
- Ask God to help you as you move forward on your "spiritual" journey.

 # THE PERSISTENT WIDOW (LUKE 18:1-8)

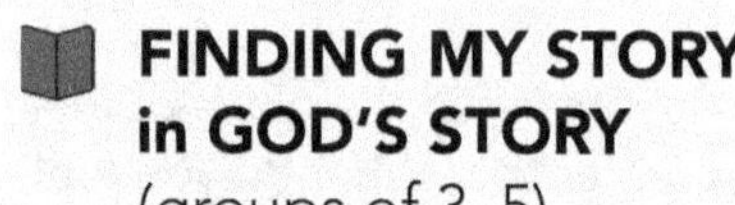 **GATHER** (all)

How did you get your way with your parents/guardians? Sulk? Beg? Bribe? Other? What worked best?

FINDING MY STORY in GOD'S STORY (groups of 3–5)

Read | Discuss Questions

1-3Jesus told them a story showing that it was necessary for them to pray consistently and never quit. He said, "There was once a judge in some city who never gave God a thought and cared nothing for people. A widow in that city kept after him: 'My rights are being violated. Protect me!'

4-5"He never gave her the time of day. But after this went on and on he said to himself, 'I care nothing what God thinks, even less what people think. But because this widow won't quit badgering me, I'd better do something and see that she gets justice—otherwise I'm going to end up beaten black-and-blue by her pounding.'"

6-8Then the Master said, "Do you hear what that judge, corrupt as he is, is saying? So what makes you think God won't step in and work justice for his chosen people, who continue to cry out for help? Won't he stick up for them? I assure you, he will. He will not drag his feet. But how much of that kind of persistent faith will the Son of Man find on the earth when he returns?"

—Luke 18:1–8 (MSG)

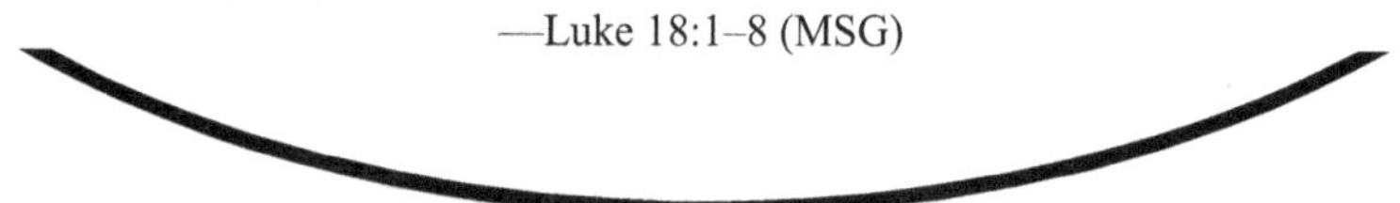

BACK STORY: Luke sets up this story by telling us Jesus' point: "Pray consistently and neve quit." His illustration involves a widow seeking justice for an unnamed offense. The Judge—described in unflattering terms—denies her request repeatedly before tiring of her showing up in court. Jesus contrasts this judge's character/begrudging response and God's response to his followers seeking justice for wrongs suffered.

1. What's most annoying about this story to you?
    - The woman's nagging
    - The judge's refusal
    - The reason the judge helped her
    - That the woman needed protection
    - Other ____________________

2. What do you think was this woman's biggest problem?
    - An arrogant judge
    - Her violated rights
    - No husband
    - No lawyer
    - Her "badgering"
    - Other ____________________

3. What do you most like about this woman?

4. Who do you think Jesus told this story for?
    - Crooked judges—to clean up their act
    - His followers with needs—to not give up praying
    - All of us—to never give up praying and trusting him
    - Other ____________________

5. How does this story speak to where you are today?
    - If at first you don't succeed—try, try again.
    - I can count on God to answer my prayers, justly.
    - Sometimes I must keep praying, trusting God will answer.
    - Other ____________________

6. When it comes to prayer, what are you most likely to do?
    - Struggle with what to say
    - Give up
    - Fall asleep
    - Hang in there
    - Other ____________________

OUR STORY (all) 

7. As you think about an issue in your life, what is the most encouraging idea coming from this story?

    ____

    ____

8. Where do you most need help?
    - More faith
    - Justice
    - Hope
    - More consistent prayer times
    - Prayer support from others
    - Other ____________________

9. How can this group support you and join you in that prayer?

IN BETWEEN (individual)

- How did the story of the widow encourage you this week?

- Where are you most wanting God to help in your life?

    Can you ask God to do that, expecting an answer?

45 THE PHARISEE & TAX COLLECTOR (LUKE 18:9-14)

During high school, did you consider yourself in the "in" crowd, or the "out" crowd? Why?

Read | Discuss Questions

[9]Then Jesus told this story to some who had great confidence in their own righteousness and scorned everyone else:

[10]"Two men went to the Temple to pray. One was a Pharisee, and the other was a despised tax collector. [11]The Pharisee stood by himself and prayed this prayer: 'I thank you, God, that I am not like other people—cheaters, sinners, adulterers. I'm certainly not like that tax collector! [12]I fast twice a week, and I give you a tenth of my income.'

[13]"But the tax collector stood at a distance and dared not even lift his eyes to heaven as he prayed. Instead, he beat his chest in sorrow, saying, 'O God, be merciful to me, for I am a sinner.' [14]I tell you, this sinner, not the Pharisee, returned home justified before God. For those who exalt themselves will be humbled, and those who humble themselves will be exalted."

—Luke 18:9–14 (NLT)

BACK STORY: Luke again tells us the theme of Jesus' lesson before recording this story, by referring to "some who had great confidence in their own righteousness and scorned everyone else." The illustration involves a **Pharisee** and a **tax collector** and their respective prayers offered in the **Temple**. The Pharisee's prayer identifies him as the self-righteous man. The tax collector, considered a traitor and sinner, approaches God in stark contrast to the Pharisee. God's approved self-posture is spelled out in the closing.

1. Imagine sitting in the temple between these two men while they prayed. What would have been going through your mind?
   - The Pharisee is really arrogant.
   - What's wrong with this tax guy?
   - Wow, talk about two opposites!
   - Other _______________

2. Why do you think the Pharisee prayed the way he did?
   - He was grateful to God.
   - He was self-centered.
   - He was trying to get God's attention.
   - He wanted others to notice him.
   - Other _______________

3. Why do you think the tax collector prayed the way he did?
   - He knew he had done wrong.
   - He wanted sympathy.
   - He didn't want others to notice him.
   - He was plea-bargaining with God.
   - Other _______________

4. What is probably the main lesson Jesus wants us to know from this story?
   - God's not a fan of self-exalting people.
   - We must honestly recognize who we are.
   - Humility is a trait of Jesus followers.
   - Other _______________

5. If the tax collector showed up to your church or this group, how would he probably be received? How about the Pharisee?
   - With suspicion
   - With a gracious welcome
   - Just like everyone else
   - Hmm ... hate to answer that
   - Other _______________

6. Compare yourself to these two men, then answer the following question: How much of the Pharisee and the tax collector do you see in yourself?

    Assign a percentage for each, that adds up to 100%.
    - I see myself as ____% Pharisee and ____% tax collector.

7. Think about those percentages (in #6) in really practical ways. For each of the following statements, which option is closer to how you see yourself?
    - I make excuses for my faults OR I take responsibility for my faults.
    - I put myself down OR I see myself like God does.
    - I have a defeated attitude OR I have a confident attitude.

8. If you could ask Jesus to make you more like the tax collector, what would you ask for?

OUR STORY (all) 

9. How do you feel about this group as a safe place to share personal, life matters?
    - Uncomfortable—not yet sure about sharing.
    - Okay—I'm willing to give it a try.
    - Happy—I need this.
    - Other ____________________

10. What could we as a group do to make it a safer place?

11. How would you like this group to pray for you this week?

IN BETWEEN (individual)

- How can you pray this week for someone who shared in the group?

- Where will you reach out to serve or bless someone?

NOTES/COMMENTS

46 THE TRIUMPHAL ENTRY (LUKE 19:28-44)

☕ GATHER (all)

How do you make your "grand entrance" when you arrive home?
A silent grunt? A big shout? A hug and kiss? Other?

"At least this is how I WANT the entrance to be when I come home!"

FINDING MY STORY in GOD'S STORY
(groups of 3–5)

Read | Discuss Questions

[28]After Jesus had said this, he went on ahead, going up to Jerusalem. [29]As he approached Bethphage and Bethany at the hill called the Mount of Olives, he sent two of his disciples, saying to them, [30]"Go to the village ahead of you, and as you enter it, you will find a colt tied there, which no one has ever ridden. Untie it and bring it here. [31]If anyone asks you, 'Why are you untying it?' say, 'The Lord needs it.'"

[32]Those who were sent ahead went and found it just as he had told them. [33]As they were untying the colt, its owners asked them, "Why are you untying the colt?"

[34]They replied, "The Lord needs it."

[35]They brought it to Jesus, threw their cloaks on the colt and put Jesus on it. [36]As he went along, people spread their cloaks on the road. [37]When he came near the place where the road goes down the Mount of Olives, the whole crowd of disciples began joyfully to praise God in loud voices for all the miracles they had seen:

[38]"Blessed is the king who comes in the name of the Lord!"

"Peace in heaven and glory in the highest!"

[39]Some of the Pharisees in the crowd said to Jesus, "Teacher, rebuke your disciples!"

[40]"I tell you," he replied, "if they keep quiet, the stones will cry out."

[41]As he approached Jerusalem and saw the city, he wept over it [42]and said, "If you, even you, had only known on this day what would bring you peace—but now it is hidden from your eyes. [43]The days will come upon you when your enemies will build an embankment against you and encircle you and hem you in on every side. [44]They will dash you to the ground, you and the children within your walls. They will not leave one stone on another, because you did not recognize the time of God's coming to you."

—Luke 19:28–44 (NIV)

*Parallel accounts:
Matthew 21:1–11, Mark 11:11–11

BACK STORY*: The final piece of Jesus' mission is close at hand. His fame has only increased as news of raising Lazarus from the dead spread far and wide. With the Feast of Passover approaching, Jesus enters Jerusalem for the last time. The crowds, swelling the city population for the Feast, line the streets and break out in shouts and cheers as Jesus passes by. Matthew's Gospel reports this as yet another fulfillment of ancient prophecy. As Jesus nears the gates, he weeps for the city and its future.

1. How would you have respond-
   ed if Jesus sent you to get a
   donkey?
   - "I could get arrested!"
   - "Must be important...."
   - "Are you kidding? How will
     we find a donkey?"
   - "No problem."
   - Other _______________

2. Put yourself in the middle of the
   shouting crowd.
   What smells surround you?
   What sounds do you hear?
   What thoughts go through your
     mind?
   Who is there?

3. Why do you think the crowd
   responded this way?
   - It was Palm Sunday.
   - Because of the miracles
     Jesus had performed.
   - They thought Jesus was the
     Messiah.
   - Jesus was coming like a king.
   - Jesus deserved their praise.
   - Other _______________

4. In the middle of the noisy
   celebration, Jesus started to
   weep. Why do you think he was
   sad when so much excitement
   surrounded him?
   - He knew how fickle people's
     loyalties are.
   - He was saddened by their
     rejection.
   - He was grieved that God's
     people missed his coming.
   - He foresaw the destruction
     of the city.

5. If Jesus rode into your commu-
   nity to announce his claim as
   the Son of God, what would be
   the most common reception?
   - Sneers and jeers
   - Joyful, heartfelt praise
   - Cold stares
   - Cruel treatment
   - Other _______________

OUR STORY (all) 

6. How would you describe your
   first encounter with Jesus, to
   this group?
   - A knight on a horse
   - Not sure I had one
   - A rabbi teaching me truth
   - A humble servant who loves
     me
   - Other _______________

7. Can you describe what you
   want Jesus to do in your life
   this week, so it can become a
   celebration?

8. How can this group pray for you
   throughout the week?

9. What can you report about an
   encounter with someone you
   served this week?

IN BETWEEN (individual)

- What are you asking and expecting Jesus to do in your life
  this week?
- Pay attention to differences you
  see.
- Thank Jesus for what he's doing
  in your life.

47 JESUS CLEARS THE TEMPLE (MARK 11:15-19)

☕ GATHER (all)

When you see something wrong happening, are you more likely to act without thinking or think without acting?

BACK STORY*: The **Temple** was a sacred place of worship. The prophet Isaiah (56:7) indicated that it was to be a house of prayer for all peoples. The outer court—the Court of the Gentiles (the only place non-Jews were allowed)—had become a place of general traffic and a marketplace for exchanging foreign currency and for purchasing animals or birds for sacrifice. Though the **Chief Priests** turned a blind eye to this misuse of the court, Jesus did not.

📖 FINDING MY STORY in GOD'S STORY (groups of 3–5)

Read | Discuss Questions

¹⁵⁻¹⁷They arrived at Jerusalem. Immediately on entering the Temple Jesus started throwing out everyone who had set up shop there, buying and selling. He kicked over the tables of the bankers and the stalls of the pigeon merchants. He didn't let anyone even carry a basket through the Temple. And then he taught them, quoting this text:

My house was designated a house of prayer for the nations;
You've turned it into a hangout for thieves.
¹⁸The high priests and religion scholars heard what was going on and plotted how they might get rid of him. They panicked, for the entire crowd was carried away by his teaching.
¹⁹At evening, Jesus and his disciples left the city.

—Mark 11:15–19 (MSG)

*Parallel accounts:
Matthew 21:12–13; Luke 19:45–48

1. If you were walking through the temple when Jesus came in, turning over tables, what would you have done?
   - Hidden behind a column
   - Run out the other door
   - Turned over a table myself
   - Started cheering with the crowd
   - Other _______________

2. Who do you think Jesus resembles in this story?
   - A club bouncer
   - A fiery prophet
   - A political activist
   - A "bull in a china shop"
   - Other _______________

3. What special or surprise insight does this story give you into Jesus?
   - Even Jesus got angry.
   - He was passionate about God's ways.
   - He didn't mind confronting wrong.
   - Other _______________

4. On a scale of 1 ("peace at any price") to 10 ("let's have it out"), how would you rate yourself on taking a stand that might lead to conflict? _______

5. What does it take for you to get involved in or take action on an issue?
   - My "stuff" is threatened
   - My family's involved
   - A moral principle is at stake
   - I think I can make a difference
   - Other _______________

6. After seeing Jesus' model, how might God be calling you to get involved in making a difference for right?
   - Reach out to community leaders
   - Live more like Jesus with my neighbors
   - Get politically active
   - Clean up my own life
   - Get to know people from a different culture
   - Other _______________

OUR STORY (all)

7. How might you begin taking action for right, this week, where you live, work, or play?

8. How do you need this group to help you?

IN BETWEEN (individual)

- Spend time asking God how you need to start acting on the issue you mentioned in #7.

- Write down specific steps you will need to take to get started.

  ____

  ____

  ____

48 WASHING THE DISCIPLES' FEET (JOHN 13:1-17)

☕ GATHER (all)

As a child, when your parents tried to get you to shower or bathe, what was your usual response?

"Like most kids, I think I loved bath time when I was little ... but resisted it more when I got older. Especially when I had to come inside from playing to get cleaned up."

BACK STORY: We find a great deal more about what transpired at this final meal with Jesus from John's Gospel. Foot washing was a normal act usually done by a servant as guests arrived from traveling the dusty or muddy roads of Palestine. Jesus uses an oversight (no one had performed this service) to teach a lesson about humility and servanthood. Peter temporarily makes a fuss about Jesus doing such a thing. Jesus corrects him and then weaves in a few extra points he wants his disciples to practice and pass on.

Read | Discuss Questions

¹Before the Passover celebration, Jesus knew that his hour had come to leave this world and return to his Father. He had loved his disciples during his ministry on earth, and now he loved them to the very end. ²It was time for supper, and the devil had already prompted Judas, son of Simon Iscariot, to betray Jesus. ³Jesus knew that the Father had given him authority over everything and that he had come from God and would return to God. ⁴So he got up from the table, took off his robe, wrapped a towel around his waist, ⁵and poured water into a basin. Then he began to wash the disciples' feet, drying them with the towel he had around him.
⁶When Jesus came to Simon Peter, Peter said to him, "Lord, are you going to wash my feet?"
⁷Jesus replied, "You don't understand now what I am doing, but someday you will."
⁸"No," Peter protested, "you will never ever wash my feet!"
Jesus replied, "Unless I wash you, you won't belong to me."

⁹Simon Peter exclaimed, "Then wash my hands and head as well, Lord, not just my feet!"
¹⁰Jesus replied, "A person who has bathed all over does not need to wash, except for the feet, to be entirely clean. And you disciples are clean, but not all of you." ¹¹For Jesus knew who would betray him. That is what he meant when he said, "Not all of you are clean."
¹²After washing their feet, he put on his robe again and sat down and asked, "Do you understand what I was doing? ¹³You call me 'Teacher' and 'Lord,' and you are right, because that's what I am. ¹⁴And since I, your Lord and Teacher, have washed your feet, you ought to wash each other's feet. ¹⁵I have given you an example to follow. Do as I have done to you. ¹⁶I tell you the truth, slaves are not greater than their master. Nor is the messenger more important than the one who sends the message. ¹⁷Now that you know these things, God will bless you for doing them.

—John 13:1–17 (NLT)

---

1. If you had been sitting at the table when Jesus came to you with his basin and towel, what would you have done?
   - Moved to the end of the line
   - Said, "My feet are ticklish"
   - Put my sandals back on
   - Stuck my feel in the bucket
   - Other ___________________

2. Why do you think Jesus washed his disciples' feet instead of calling for a servant or telling one of the disciples to do it?
   - To model humility
   - To show servant leadership
   - To demonstrate his deep love for them
   - Other ___________________

3. Verse 3 tells us that Jesus knew his source of authority, where he was from, and where he was going. How do you think that understanding gave him the ability to do a "servant's" task?
   - He knew he was going to wash his hands soon.
   - He didn't need to worry about his reputation.

- I don't see how it made any difference in his actions.
- Other _______________

How might you live differently if you were certain of your source of authority, where you were from, where you were going?

4. Why do you think Jesus said, "Unless I wash you, you won't belong to me"?
   - He didn't want to share a room with anyone with dirty feet.
   - To be his follower, we must depend on him.
   - We will always need Jesus to make us clean inside.
   - Unless we're servants like Jesus, we can't be his disciples.
   - Other _______________

5. What might Jesus mean when he tells the disciples they should wash one another's feet?
   - Literally, wash each other's feet
   - Be willing to do the "dirty work"
   - Take care of each other
   - Be willing to serve others
   - Other _______________

6. What task do you do that is most like "washing feet"?
   - Take the trash out
   - Clean the bathroom
   - Change diapers/wash kids
   - Yard work
   - Other _______________

7. Who has been a great "foot washer" to you?

____

How have they done it? What can you learn from them?

OUR STORY (all)

8. What might it mean for you to practice foot-washing in your daily relationships?
   - Do unpleasant tasks willingly
   - Spend more time with family
   - Help in my neighborhood
   - Serve with no strings attached
   - Do things that aren't "my job"
   - Other _______________

9. What one thing will you do this week to follow Jesus' example of serving?

____

____

10. How can this group help you be accountable to serve this week?

IN BETWEEN (individual)

- Have you started the commitment you made in #9?
- Ask God to help you do it as a model of Jesus to those you serve.
- Jot down notes of what happens when you serve.

49 THE LAST SUPPER (MATTHEW 26:20-30)

 **GATHER** (all)

Did you have regular mealtimes when you were a child?

If so, who usually sat at the table?
If not, where/when was your favorite mealtime?

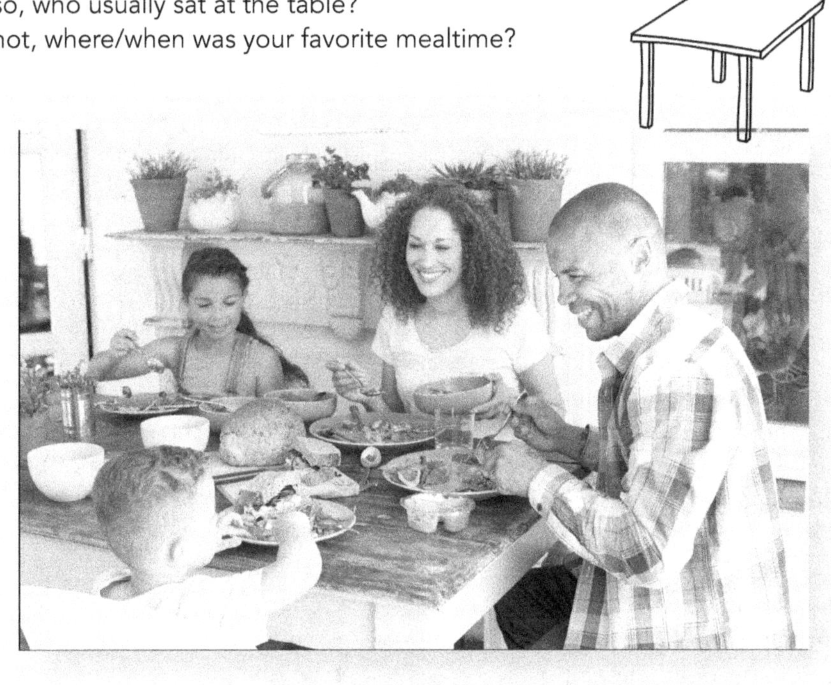

"We ate together whenever we could. We didn't always sit in the same places, so it was a kind of game to see who would sit where each time."

Read | Discuss Questions

[17]On the first day of the Festival of Unleavened Bread, the disciples came to Jesus and asked, "Where do you want us to make preparations for you to eat the Passover?"
[18]He replied, "Go into the city to a certain man and tell him, 'The Teacher says: My appointed time is near. I am going to celebrate the Passover with my disciples at your house.'" [19]So the disciples did as Jesus had directed them and prepared the Passover.
[20]When evening came, Jesus was reclining at the table with the Twelve. [21]And while they were eating, he said, "Truly I tell you, one of you will betray me."
[22]They were very sad and began to say to him one after the other, "Surely you don't mean me, Lord?"
[23]Jesus replied, "The one who has dipped his hand into the bowl with me will betray me. [24]The Son of Man will go just as it is written about him. But woe to that man who betrays the Son of Man! It would be better for him if he had not been born."
[25]Then Judas, the one who would betray him, said, "Surely you don't mean me, Rabbi?"
Jesus answered, "You have said so."
[26]While they were eating, Jesus took bread, and when he had given thanks, he broke it and gave it to his disciples, saying, "Take and eat; this is my body."
[27]Then he took a cup, and when he had given thanks, he gave it to them, saying, "Drink from it, all of you. [28]This is my blood of the covenant, which is poured out for many for the forgiveness of sins. [29]I tell you, I will not drink from this fruit of the vine from now on until that day when I drink it new with you in my Father's kingdom."
[30]When they had sung a hymn, they went out to the Mount of Olives.
—Matthew 26:17–30 (NIV)

BACK STORY*: Two Jewish celebrations are at hand (**Passover** and the **Feast** of Unleavened Bread), and the plot against Jesus is coming together. On the eve of these celebrations, Jesus hosts a last meal and teaching time with his disciples before his death. Reading all four Gospels helps us discover what occurred at this meal Christians celebrate as the Last Supper. Jesus prepares his disciples for what will happen over the next 24 hours and forever transforms the meaning of Passover for Christians.

*Parallel accounts: Mark 14:17–25; Luke 22:7–20; John 13:1–2

1. As you read this "last supper" story, what kinds of emotions do you think Jesus was feeling?
    - Nostalgia
    - Real sadness
    - Happiness to be with his friends
    - Wishing he didn't have to be there
    - Other _______________

2. Why do you think Jesus wanted to have this supper with his disciples?
    - Meals had always been important times to him.
    - To share some final teaching.
    - To give his disciples a symbol

of his death, as a way to remember him.

- Other _______________________

3. Before Jesus served the bread and wine, he made a clear point of naming Judas as his betrayer. Why do you think he did it in front of the other disciples?
   - So they'd understand that he was serious.
   - To help them get a more complete picture of what was about to happen.
   - To give Judas a chance to change his mind under peer pressure.
   - Other _______________________

4. How might pointing out his betrayer set the stage for the broken bread and wine we celebrate as Holy Communion (or Eucharist)?

5. Where do you most deeply connect to this part of Jesus' story?
   - Celebrating Holy Communion is really important to me.
   - I sometimes feel like Judas, sneaking away.
   - Sometimes I'm spiritually sad, like the other disciples.
   - I've not yet connected to the meaning of all this.
   - Other _______________________

6. What new or growing understanding about Jesus do you think you're learning from this story? What difference might that understanding make in you/your life?

OUR STORY (all)

7. If you participate in Communion somewhere, how might you be better prepared to participate in it after discussing this story?
   - I gained a deeper appreciation of its significance.
   - I'll watch what the leader does with the bread and wine.
   - I'll pay closer attention to the words of the service.
   - Other _______________________

8. If you're able, get some bread and juice/wine. Have one group member re-read verses 26–28. As each part is read, break the bread and hold up the juice at the appropriate time. Then each person take a piece of bread and dip it in the wine/juice. All eat at the same time.

9. Close with the group saying/praying "Thank you, Jesus" in unison.

IN BETWEEN (individual)

- Spend time this week jotting notes about what you remember from the Last Supper Bible story.

- Who will you serve, encourage, or bless this week?

50 JESUS IN GETHSEMANE (MARK 14:32-42)

Choose one:
- When did you fall asleep at an embarrassing moment?
- If you were facing a crisis, what three friends would you ask to stay with you?

"One of my first times hanging out with my girlfriend (now wife), we drove to Miami and I fell asleep in the car. She took photos of me. After that, every time we rode in the car together and I'd fall asleep she would take pictures of me as proof!"

Read | Discuss Questions

[32-34]They came to an area called Gethsemane. Jesus told his disciples, "Sit here while I pray." He took Peter, James, and John with him. He plunged into a sinkhole of dreadful agony. He told them, "I feel bad enough right now to die. Stay here and keep vigil with me."

[35-36]Going a little ahead, he fell to the ground and prayed for a way out: "Papa, Father, you can—can't you?—get me out of this. Take this cup away from me. But please, not what I want—what do you want?"

[37-38]He came back and found them sound asleep. He said to Peter, "Simon, you went to sleep on me? Can't you stick it out with me a single hour? Stay alert, be in prayer, so you don't enter the danger zone without even knowing it. Don't be naive. Part of you is eager, ready for anything in God; but another part is as lazy as an old dog sleeping by the fire."

[39-40]He then went back and prayed the same prayer. Returning, he again found them sound asleep. They simply couldn't keep their eyes open, and they didn't have a plausible excuse.

[41-42]He came back a third time and said, "Are you going to sleep all night? No—you've slept long enough. Time's up. The Son of Man is about to be betrayed into the hands of sinners. Get up. Let's get going. My betrayer has arrived."

—Mark 14:32–42 (MSG)

*Parallel accounts: Matthew 26:36–46; Luke 22:40–46; John 18:1

BACK STORY*: After the Last Supper and a final mentoring time together, Jesus and the disciples retreat to an olive garden outside Jerusalem (Gethsemane). Jesus takes Peter, James, and John apart to pray. Three times he goes off a short distance by himself. Though sleep overtook the three, years later they remember the way he addressed God that night, and the overwhelming agony in his voice as he wrestled with what he knew lay ahead.

1. Write 4 or 5 words that come to your mind to describe this scene in the garden.

   _______________ _______________

   _______________ _______________

   ____

2. Why do you think Jesus went to Gethsemane to pray?

- It's where he often went.
- He was stressed; needing strength and guidance.
- He wanted to give his disciples an example.
- It was his last chance to ask God for a different plan.
- Other _______________

3. Why was it important to take Peter, James, and John along?
    - He needed their support.
    - They were the three closest disciples to him.
    - He wanted them to pray with him.
    - Other _______________

4. If you were watching this experience from a nearby boulder, what would you say was the hardest part for Jesus?
    - Being let down by his friends
    - Preparing for the cross
    - Knowing what was coming
    - Other _______________

5. If you pray, what are things you often pray for?
    - Good health
    - Help!
    - Safety
    - God's will in my life
    - Other _______________

6. Think about the various areas of your life. What area would you describe as "part of me is eager…part is as lazy as a dog"?
    - Healthy eating
    - Regular exercise
    - Finding time to pray
    - Doing Bible reading
    - Quality family time
    - Completing chores/projects
    - Other _______________

7. Rank these items—one (1) being the greatest struggle for you.
    - ____ Trying to figure out what God wants from me
    - ____ Doing what I know God wants
    - ____ Standing alone without others' support
    - ____ Watching someone I love go through struggles
    - ____ Other _______________

8. If you've found help in your life struggles, where do you usually get it?
    - The Bible
    - I usually struggle alone
    - Praying
    - Good friends
    - Other _______________

OUR STORY (all)

9. How does this story relate to an issue you're currently facing?
    - It's okay for me to ask God to change my situation.
    - Part of prayer is becoming willing to follow God's plan.
    - God's plan for my life may not be easy, but it is best.
    - "Part of me is eager…part is as lazy as an old dog."
    - Other _______________

10. How can the group pray for needs in your life?

IN BETWEEN (individual)

- Spend some time asking God to show you direction for your life.
- Write down notes of what comes to your mind that is affirming to you.

51 JESUS ARRESTED (MATTHEW 26:47-56)

 **GATHER** (all)

Choose one:

- Who is your favorite adventure hero? How do they respond to danger?

- If you could call a group of angels to do one thing for you, what would it be?

BACK STORY*: The plot to take Jesus unfolds in rapid succession. Afraid of the crowds who stand in awe of Jesus' teaching and miracles, the Jewish leaders conspire with Judas to take him at night. Armed with swords and clubs, a small army of Temple guards arrive in the olive grove. Jesus maintains control of the commotion. He calls Judas a friend, mocks the idea of his leading a rebellion, calms Peter down (see John 18:10–11), and watches as the disciples exit.

 **FINDING MY STORY in GOD'S STORY** (groups of 3–5)

Read | Discuss Questions

[47]And even as Jesus said this, Judas, one of the twelve disciples, arrived with a crowd of men armed with swords and clubs. They had been sent by the leading priests and elders of the people. [48]The traitor, Judas, had given them a prearranged signal: "You will know which one to arrest when I greet him with a kiss." [49]So Judas came straight to Jesus. "Greetings, Rabbi!" he exclaimed and gave him the kiss.

[50]Jesus said, "My friend, go ahead and do what you have come for."

Then the others grabbed Jesus and arrested him. [51]But one of the men with Jesus pulled out his sword and struck the high priest's slave, slashing off his ear.

[52]"Put away your sword," Jesus told him. "Those who use the sword will die by the sword. [53]Don't you realize that I could ask my Father for thousands of angels to protect us, and he would send them instantly? [54]But if I did, how would the Scriptures be fulfilled that describe what must happen now?" [55]Then Jesus said to the crowd, "Am I some dangerous revolutionary, that you come with swords and clubs to arrest me? Why didn't you arrest me in the Temple? I was there teaching every day. [56]But this is all happening to fulfill the words of the prophets as recorded in the Scriptures." At that point, all the disciples deserted him and fled.

—Matthew 26:47–56 (NLT)

*Parallel accounts: Mark 14:43–50; Luke 22: 47–53

1. As one of Jesus' disciples, what would you have done when this armed mob appeared with Judas?
   - Run for my life
   - Jumped between Judas and Jesus
   - Grabbed a sword like Peter
   - Tried to become a negotiator
   - Other _______________

2. Why do you think Jesus is the only calm one here?

3. What do you think was the main reason that the disciples deserted Jesus?
   - Their leader appeared defeated.
   - They panicked.
   - Jesus wasn't the kind of Messiah they wanted.
   - Other _______________

4. What do you suppose was the hardest part of this arrest, for Jesus?
   - Betrayal by a friend
   - Desertion by the disciples
   - Knowing what was coming
   - Knowing he could call for rescue but didn't
   - Other _______________

5. How would your spouse or best friend rate you in handling a crisis?
   - I'm cool like Jesus.
   - I'm hot-headed like Peter.
   - I panic like the disciples.
   - I'm conniving like Judas.
   - Other _______________

Give an example.

6. How do you deal with being let down or betrayed?
   - Go for exercise
   - Punch a pillow
   - Ask God for help
   - Try to understand the other person
   - Other _______________

OUR STORY (all) 

7. On a scale of 1 (low) to 5 (high), how would you rate yourself on the following statements?
   - ____ I'm always loyal to my friends.
   - ____ My friends are always loyal to me.
   - ____ I try to always be loyal to Jesus.

8. Report briefly what you're learning about God's direction for you, since the last meeting.

9. How can this group help you in the coming week?

IN BETWEEN (individual)

- Where will you serve like Jesus this week? Who will you serve?

- Write some notes about what happens and what you learn.

52 PETER DISOWNS JESUS (MARK 14:66-72)

 **GATHER** (all)

Who do you admire because they made a comeback after a defeat, injury or other setback?

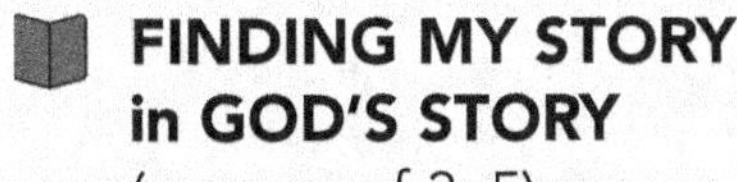 **FINDING MY STORY in GOD'S STORY**
(groups of 3–5)

BACK STORY*: As the trial before the High Priest and the **Sanhedrin** takes place, Peter is recognized in the courtyard. Earlier that evening, Jesus—quoting Zechariah 13:7—had told his disciples they would all abandon him. An overconfident Peter declared that would never happen—a sentiment echoed by the other disciples (Mark 14:31). Having already run away once, Peter distances himself further when bystanders charge him with being with Jesus. The crow of a rooster reminds him of Jesus' words.

*Parallel accounts: Matthew 26:58, 69–75; Luke 22:54-62; John 18:15–18, 25–27

Read | Discuss Questions

66While Peter was below in the courtyard, one of the servant girls of the high priest came by. 67When she saw Peter warming himself, she looked closely at him.

"You also were with that Nazarene, Jesus," she said. 68But he denied it. "I don't know or understand what you're talking about," he said, and went out into the entryway.

69When the servant girl saw him there, she said again to those standing around, "This fellow is one of them." 70Again he denied it.

After a little while, those standing near said to Peter, "Surely you are one of them, for you are a Galilean." 71He began to call down curses, and he swore to them, "I don't know this man you're talking about."

72Immediately the rooster crowed the second time. Then Peter remembered the word Jesus had spoken to him: "Before the rooster crows twice you will disown me three times." And he broke down and wept.

—Mark 14:66–72 (NIV)

1. If you'd followed the crowd arresting Jesus, where would you have wanted to watch from?
    *   As close to Jesus as possible
    *   Just close enough to hear, far enough to avoid being seen
    *   Next to Peter in the courtyard
    *   I wouldn't have followed
    *   Other _______________

2. Why do you think Peter went from the brave talker to denying he knew Jesus?
    *   Momentary insanity
    *   Fear of standing out
    *   Afraid he'd end up like Jesus
    *   Other _______________

3. If you were producing this story as a movie, how would you title it?

    ____

    ____

4. When have you, like Peter, felt like you failed?
    *   When I lost my job
    *   Not following God
    *   When we had family issues
    *   When I struggled financially
    *   When I didn't stand up for what's right
    *   Other _______________

5. How would you describe your reaction when you feel like you've let someone down?
    *   Kick myself for days
    *   Talk to a friend
    *   Try to learn from it
    *   Other _______________

6. What has helped you to get through feelings of failure?
    *   Taking time alone
    *   Having a good cry
    *   Analyzing what went wrong
    *   Asking God for help
    *   Accepting responsibility
    *   Other _______________

OUR STORY (all)

7. Think back to a time (like #4) you consider a failure. How has your life changed because of it?
    *   I'm more determined.
    *   I'm more humble.
    *   I'm more realistic.
    *   I don't want to try again.
    *   I'm more sensitive to others' pain.
    *   Other _______________

8. Complete the sentence: "I want to thank _______________ for sharing your story with us today."

9. How do you need this group to pray for you this week?

IN BETWEEN (individual)

Find a person to encourage this week.

53 JESUS BEFORE PILATE (MARK 15:1-15)

If you could choose the role you'd play in a high-profile court case, what would it be: judge, jury, expert witness, defender, prosecutor, etc.? Why that role?

"My parents used to tell me I should be a lawyer. I guess that means I argued a lot! But, that's the role I would pick. I love to debate difficult questions and try to get people to see my point of view."

BACK STORY*: The **Sanhedrin's** limited governing authority did not include capital punishment, so the Jewish leaders take Jesus to Governor **Pontius Pilate** and present their list of charges (reached in the early morning hours). Pilate, though surprised by Jesus' lack of response, is reticent to convict because he sees through the bogus charges against him. Pilate offers Jesus another option, but, in the end, gives in to the crowd to keep the peace.

*Parallel accounts: Matthew 27:1–26, Luke 23:1–25

Read | Discuss Questions

[1]Very early in the morning, the chief priests, with the elders, the teachers of the law and the whole Sanhedrin, made their plans. So they bound Jesus, led him away and handed him over to Pilate.
[2]"Are you the king of the Jews?" asked Pilate.

"You have said so," Jesus replied.
[3]The chief priests accused him of many things. [4]So again Pilate asked him, "Aren't you going to answer? See how many things they are accusing you of."
[5]But Jesus still made no reply, and Pilate was amazed.
[6]Now it was the custom at the festival to release a prisoner whom the people requested. [7]A man called Barabbas was in prison with the insurrectionists who had committed murder in the uprising. [8]The crowd came up and asked Pilate to do for them what he usually did.

[9]"Do you want me to release to you the king of the Jews?" asked Pilate, [10]knowing it was out of self-interest that the chief priests had handed Jesus over to him. [11]But the chief priests stirred up the crowd to have Pilate release Barabbas instead.
[12]"What shall I do, then, with the one you call the king of the Jews?" Pilate asked them.
[13]"Crucify him!" they shouted.
[14]"Why? What crime has he committed?" asked Pilate.

But they shouted all the louder, "Crucify him!"
[15]Wanting to satisfy the crowd, Pilate released Barabbas to them. He had Jesus flogged, and handed him over to be crucified.

—Mark 15:1–15 (NIV)

1. Remember back to a time when someone accused you of something you didn't do. How did you react?
   - Wrote a response in the local news
   - Confronted them privately
   - Can't remember a time
   - Asked my friends to defend me
   - Other ______________________

2. What part of this story is the most frustrating to you?
   - That Jesus was so silent
   - That the crowd turned on Jesus
   - That a murderer was released instead of Jesus
   - That Jesus allowed this to happen when he could have escaped
   - Other ______________________

3. Why do you think Jesus didn't defend himself to Pilate?
   - His words had been so twisted, there was no point in speaking.
   - He trusted God's plan.
   - The minds of his accusers were made up.
   - The Old Testament prophesied about the Messiah's silence.
   - Other ______________________

4. Which character in this story do you most relate to? Why?
   - Pilate—wanting to keep people happy
   - Jesus—acting on his convictions; suffering the consequences
   - The crowd—easily swayed by others
   - Barabbas—guilty, yet released
   - Religious leaders—manipulating the scene
   - Other ___________________

5. Who do you think ended up the biggest winner in this part of the story?
   Who ended up the biggest loser? Why?
   - Pilate
   - Jesus
   - The Sanhedrin
   - The crowd
   - Barabbas
   - Me

6. When, if ever, did Jesus become more than just a word to you?
   - As a child
   - Just recently
   - I don't know that it has
   - Other ___________________

OUR STORY (all) 

7. What did you learn from this story that you'll spend time reflecting on in the next week?

   ____

   ____

8. How should this group pray for you this week?

9. Who did you try to encourage in the last week? What response did you get from them? What did you learn from them?

IN BETWEEN (individual)

- Set aside time to re-read this story. Read out loud if you can—so you can hear the words. Ask God to teach you more about his love through the story. **Write notes** about what comes to your mind.

- Focus on looking for someone who serves you, and finding a way to serve them back (such as a cashier or restaurant server).

 GATHER (all)

Can you remember being penalized for something you didn't do?

What's the story behind it?

BACK STORY*:

Crucifixion was a particularly cruel punishment. Victims could suffer for days before dying of asphyxiation. Jesus, weakened from a severe beating, carries his own cross to the execution site. Pilate, in a parting insult to the Jewish leadership, hangs a sign that declares Jesus the King of the Jews. Jesus' mother, one disciple, and others from Galilee join the crowd of onlookers. Jesus makes seven brief statements, then gives up his life and dies within a few short hours. John gives details that only an eyewitness could have known.

FINDING MY STORY in GOD'S STORY (groups of 3–5)

Read | Discuss Questions

[16-19]Pilate caved in to their demand. He turned him over to be crucified.

They took Jesus away. Carrying his cross, Jesus went out to the place called Skull Hill (the name in Hebrew is Golgotha), where they crucified him, and with him two others, one on each side, Jesus in the middle. Pilate wrote a sign and had it placed on the cross. It read:

JESUS THE NAZARENE

THE KING OF THE JEWS

[20-21]Many of the Jews read the sign because the place where Jesus was crucified was right next to the city. It was written in Hebrew, Latin, and Greek. The Jewish high priests objected. "Don't write," they said to Pilate, "'The King of the Jews.' Make it, 'This man said, "I am the King of the Jews."'"

[22]Pilate said, "What I've written, I've written."

[23-24]When they crucified him, the Roman soldiers took his clothes and divided them up four ways, to each soldier a fourth. But his robe was seamless, a single piece of weaving, so they said to each other, "Let's not tear it up. Let's throw dice to see who gets it." This confirmed the Scripture that said, "They divided up my clothes among them and threw dice for my coat." (The soldiers validated the Scriptures!)

24-27While the soldiers were looking after themselves, Jesus' mother, his aunt, Mary the wife of Clopas, and Mary Magdalene stood at the foot of the cross. Jesus saw his mother and the disciple he loved standing near her. He said to his mother, "Woman, here is your son." Then to the disciple, "Here is your mother." From that moment the disciple accepted her as his own mother. 28Jesus, seeing that everything had been completed so that the Scripture record might also be complete, then said, "I'm thirsty." 29-30A jug of sour wine was standing by. Someone put a sponge soaked with the wine on a javelin and lifted it to his mouth. After he took the wine, Jesus said, "It's done . . . complete." Bowing his head, he offered up his spirit.

—John 19:16–30 (MSG)

*Parallel accounts: Matthew 2:32–55; Mark 15: 21–41; Luke 23:26–49

---

1. Which symbol best illustrates Jesus' crucifixion for you?
   - Storm clouds blocking the sun—a most dreadful day
   - Sunset—the end of an old era
   - Sunrise—hope of a new day
   - Other

2. Try to imagine being Jesus' mother. She had known this day was coming since before Jesus was born. How do you think you would have handled these moments, now that they were real?
   - Totally confused
   - Not really surprised
   - In deep grief
   - Angry at the injustice
   - Other ______________________

3. If you were standing next to Mary, what would you want to say or do?

4. Which part of this scene hits your emotions the hardest?
   - The callousness of the soldiers
   - The loyalty of Jesus' mother and friends
   - Jesus' pain
   - The attitudes of the religious leaders
   - Jesus, in his last moments, caring for his mother
   - Other ______________________

5. Think about a time(s) when you were more like the soldiers who "played games" at the cross than one of Jesus' friends.

   How did it show up in your life?
   - When I was selfish
   - Can't think of a time
   - When I hurt other people
   - When I didn't take Jesus seriously
   - Other ______________________

6. Jesus told John to care for his mother. Can you think of a bigger principle that Jesus might want his disciples (and us) to learn from his statement?
   - Take care of each other
   - No one is alone
   - Care for those in need
   - Other ______________________

7. How does it make you feel, if you stop to think about Jesus dying for you?
    - Amazed
    - Not sure
    - Grateful
    - Guilty
    - Loved
    - Uncomfortable
    - Other _________________

OUR STORY (all) 

8. What gift did you receive from this story or someone in the group today?

9. How might you be different this week, after discussing the Crucifixion story?

10. How do you need this group to support you this week?

IN BETWEEN (individual)

- Spend some quiet time pondering the Crucifixion story, and its meaning for you.

- Do you sense more grief or more gratitude?

- **Write down** your thoughts. Tell God what you're thinking about.

NOTES/COMMENTS

55 JESUS' RESURRECTION (LUKE 24:1-12)

 **GATHER** (all)

Choose one:

- How did you celebrate Easter when you were a kid?

- What is the best news you've ever heard; so amazing you couldn't believe it was true?

BACK STORY*: Jesus' Resurrection is the foundational truth of Christian belief (1 Corinthians 15:17). The fact that the women who showed up at the tomb were surprised—and that others reacted to their announcement with disbelief—indicates they didn't expect to see Jesus alive after he was pronounced dead. Peter and John run to the tomb and see the grave clothes; only then do they begin to wonder whether what Jesus foretold had really happened! Fearful of a resurrection story, Roman authorities paid the guards to lie (Matthew 28:12).

 **FINDING MY STORY in GOD'S STORY** (groups of 3–5)

Read | Discuss Questions

[1]But very early on Sunday morning[a] the women went to the tomb, taking the spices they had prepared. [2]They found that the stone had been rolled away from the entrance. [3]So they went in, but they didn't find the body of the Lord Jesus. [4]As they stood there puzzled, two men suddenly appeared to them, clothed in dazzling robes. [5]The women were terrified and bowed with their faces to the ground. Then the men asked, "Why are you looking among the dead for someone who is alive? [6]He isn't here! He is risen from the dead! Remember what he told you back in Galilee, [7]that the Son of Man must be betrayed into the hands of sinful men and be crucified, and that he would rise again on the third day." [8]Then they remembered that he had said this. [9]So they rushed back from the tomb to tell his eleven disciples—and everyone else—what had happened. [10]It was Mary Magdalene, Joanna, Mary the mother of James, and several other women who told the apostles what had happened. [11]But the story sounded like nonsense to the men, so they didn't believe it. [12]However, Peter jumped up and ran to the tomb to look. Stooping, he peered in and saw the empty linen wrappings; then he went home again, wondering what had happened.

—Luke 24:1–12 (NLT)

1. If you'd been helping the women take the spices to the tomb, what do you think you would have talked about on the way?
   - How to move the rock door
   - Why the sun was so late coming up
   - Where had all the male disciples gone?
   - Mostly just walked in silence
   - Other ___________________

2. Imagine finding the stone moved, and going inside, finding no body. What questions would have immediately come to your mind?
   - Where's the giant that moved that stone?
   - Who's going to believe this?
   - How do we get our stories straight?
   - Who said it couldn't get worse?
   - Other ___________________

3. When men in dazzling robes appeared to announce the resurrection, the scene immediately changed. Can you remember a time when you went from deep grief to high hope? What was happening to bring you hope?

4. When the women told the news to the disciples, the males didn't believe it. Why do you think they didn't take the women seriously?
   - They were women; not considered reliable sources.
   - The story was too amazing to be taken seriously.
   - They were in such deep grief—they couldn't remember Jesus' words.
   - Other ___________________

5. If you tried to explain Jesus' resurrection to the people around you (family, coworkers, neighbors), do you think they'd respond more like the women ... or more like the eleven disciples? Why?

6. When you seriously think about Jesus' resurrection, what attitudes do you experience?
   - Wow, amazing!
   - I'm not sure what to think.
   - Sounds too good to be true.
   - I'd like to believe.
   - It has changed my life.
   - Other ___________________

OUR STORY (all) 

7. What big question do you wish Jesus would answer about his resurrection?

   How might his answer make a difference in your life this week?

8. How would you like the group to pray with you this week?

IN BETWEEN (individual)

Where are you going to serve this week?

56 JESUS APPEARS TO MARY MAGDALENE (JOHN 20:1-18)

 **GATHER** (all)

When was the last time you were at a cemetary? How did you feel there?

"When we buried my mother. The time before that was when we buried my father. We all drove to the cemetary in Michigan."

BACK STORY*: Mary Magdalene
ventures to the tomb alone, still confused over
Jesus' missing body. Through tears, she looks in the
tomb ... and sees two beings where the body had been.
They question what she is looking for, perhaps to help her
remember what Jesus had promised. Nothing registers until
she hears a voice call her by name. Jesus tells her what to say
to the disciples, and the world's first witness of the risen Jesus
hurries out and reports who she has seen.

FINDING MY STORY in GOD'S STORY
(groups of 3–5)

[1-2] Early in the morning on the first day of the week, while it was still dark, Mary Magdalene came to the tomb and saw that the stone was moved away from the entrance. She ran at once to Simon Peter and the other disciple, the one Jesus loved, breathlessly panting, "They took the Master from the tomb. We don't know where they've put him."

[3-10] Peter and the other disciple left immediately for the tomb. They ran, neck and neck. The other disciple got to the tomb first, outrunning Peter. Stooping to look in, he saw the pieces of linen cloth lying there, but he didn't go in. Simon Peter arrived after him, entered the tomb, observed the linen cloths lying there, and the kerchief used to cover his head not lying with the linen cloths but separate, neatly folded by itself. Then the other disciple, the one who had gotten there first, went into the tomb, took one look at the evidence, and believed. No one yet knew from the Scripture that he had to rise from the dead. The disciples then went back home.

[11-13] But Mary stood outside the tomb weeping. As she wept, she knelt to look into the tomb and saw two angels sitting there, dressed in white, one at the head, the other at the foot of where Jesus' body had been laid. They said to her, "Woman, why do you weep?"

[13-14] "They took my Master," she said, "and I don't know where they put him." After she said this, she turned away and saw Jesus standing there. But she didn't recognize him.

[15] Jesus spoke to her, "Woman, why do you weep? Who are you looking for?"
She, thinking that he was the gardener, said, "Mister, if you took him, tell me where you put him so I can care for him."

[16] Jesus said, "Mary."
Turning to face him, she said in Hebrew, "Rabboni!" meaning "Teacher!"

[17] Jesus said, "Don't cling to me, for I have not yet ascended to the Father. Go to my brothers and tell them, 'I ascend to my Father and your Father, my God and your God.'"

[18] Mary Magdalene went, telling the news to the disciples: "I saw the Master!" And she told them everything he said to her.

—John 20:1–18 (MSG)

*Parallel account: Mark 16:9–11

---

1. Put yourself in the role of a news videographer, watching this scene. So much action as people ran back and forth—then Mary's moment alone with Jesus. What would you have photographed to capture this story? Why?

2. Imagine being a woman in Mary's culture—the first to see Jesus; given the assignment to start spreading the "resurrection word." What emotions do you think you'd have felt?

- Up and down—grief to amazing joy
- Knowing I mattered, to the One who mattered
- Puzzled at how I could be in the center of such a story
- Wondering how they'd write about me in the Bible
- Frustration that the guys will never believe me
- Other ___________________

3. Re-read verses 3–10. What is surprising to you about the interaction between John ("the

other disciple") and Peter?

- How they each respond to the empty tomb
- That they go home, rather than back to tell the other disciples

4. Mary didn't leave with John and Peter. Instead she stayed to absorb what was happening. Why do you think Mary didn't recognize Jesus at first?
   - His appearance was different.
   - She was blinded by grief.
   - She couldn't believe the angels' message was true.
   - He wasn't where she expected him to be.
   - Other ________________

5. What do you learn about Jesus from his response to Mary?
   - He cares enough to know my name.
   - He'll meet me where I hurt.
   - He has a mission/purpose for me.
   - Other ________________

6. When was the last time you really needed to cry?
   - Death of a family member
   - A good movie
   - So excited I couldn't speak
   - Other ________________

   What was the situation?

7. If you could choose a place for Jesus to show himself to you, what would be the setting?
   - In work relationships
   - During loneliness
   - When I'm meditating on a Bible reading

- When I've lost a loved one
- When I'm in nature
- Other ________________

OUR STORY (all) 

8. After discussing this story of Mary, what is one big thought that you can use right now?

9. Where do you need Jesus to show up in your life this week?

10. How can the group help you this week?

IN BETWEEN (individual)

- Talk to God about where you need help this week.

- Make sure to **jot down some notes** of what you see God doing in your life.

- Who will you serve or encourage this week?

  ____

- What will you do? Be ready to report in at the next group meeting.

171

57 ON THE ROAD TO EMMAUS (LUKE 24:13-35)

☕ GATHER (all)

Choose one:

- When you're emotionally down, do you want to be alone or with others?

- Where's your favorite place to go when you need to get away and think?

"A short walk from my house is a quiet park beside a lake. I like to sit on one of the benches and think ... or just take in the view."

BACK STORY*:

Two persons struggle to make sense of what happened three days earlier, as Jesus catches up to them on the road. Preventing them from recognizing him, Jesus asks why they are sad and what they are discussing. They confess that, even though two **disciples** confirm the tomb was empty, and a woman reports seeing Jesus alive, they are discouraged and headed home. (Perhaps because it was a *woman* that saw Jesus?) Only after Jesus takes them through a review of the Old Testament and then prays in their hearing does it finally click who he is.

Read | Discuss Questions

¹³That same day two of Jesus' followers were walking to the village of Emmaus, seven miles[a] from Jerusalem. ¹⁴As they walked along they were talking about everything that had happened. ¹⁵As they talked and discussed these things, Jesus himself suddenly came and began walking with them. ¹⁶But God kept them from recognizing him.

¹⁷He asked them, "What are you discussing so intently as you walk along?"

They stopped short, sadness written across their faces. ¹⁸Then one of them, Cleopas, replied, "You must be the only person in Jerusalem who hasn't heard about all the things that have happened there the last few days."

¹⁹"What things?" Jesus asked.

"The things that happened to Jesus, the man from Nazareth," they said. "He was a prophet who did powerful miracles, and he was a mighty teacher in the eyes of God and all the people. ²⁰But our leading priests and other religious leaders handed him over to be condemned to death, and they crucified him. ²¹We had hoped he was the Messiah who had come to rescue Israel. This all happened three days ago.

²²"Then some women from our group of his followers were at his tomb early this morning, and they came back with an amazing report. ²³They said his body was missing, and they had seen angels who told them Jesus is alive! ²⁴Some of our men ran out to see, and sure enough, his body was gone, just as the women had said."

²⁵Then Jesus said to them, "You foolish people! You find it so hard to believe all that the prophets wrote in the Scriptures. ²⁶Wasn't it clearly predicted that the Messiah would have to suffer all these things before entering his glory?" ²⁷Then Jesus took them through the writings of Moses and all the prophets, explaining from all the Scriptures the things concerning himself.

²⁸By this time they were nearing Emmaus and the end of their journey. Jesus acted as if he were going on, ²⁹but they begged him, "Stay the night with us, since it is getting late." So he went home with them. ³⁰As they sat down to eat, he took the bread and blessed it. Then he broke it and gave it to them. ³¹Suddenly, their eyes were opened, and they recognized him. And at that moment he disappeared!

³²They said to each other, "Didn't our hearts burn within us as he talked with us on the road and explained the Scriptures to us?" ³³And within the hour they were on their way back to Jerusalem. There they found the eleven disciples and the others who had gathered with them, ³⁴who said, "The Lord has really risen! He appeared to Peter." ³⁵Then the two from Emmaus told their story of how Jesus had appeared to them as they were walking along the road, and how they had recognized him as he was breaking the bread.—Luke 24:13–35 (NLT)

*Parallel account: Mark 16:12–3

---

1. If you had been one of these Jesus-followers, why might you have left Jerusalem?
    - Too many people in the house with the other disciples
    - Fear—afraid for our lives
    - Overload—needed an emotional break
    - Despair—lost our hope
    - Other ______________________

2. Why do you think the two people were kept from recognizing Jesus?
    - To keep them from getting too excited, too soon

- So they'd pay attention to his teaching
- They'd want Jesus to carry them the seven miles
- Other _______________

3. What about the bread-breaking do you think helped "open their eyes"?
   - Meals are good times with friends.
   - Jesus had finished teaching them.
   - It reminded them of the Last Supper with him.
   - All of a sudden, everything made sense.
   - Other _______________

4. What might be a way that Jesus would show up "alongside" you?
   - Sensing God's presence when I pray
   - Talking with someone who cares
   - Sometimes when I read the Bible
   - Not sure how I'd know
   - When I'm worshipping with a group
   - Other _______________

5. If you could get Jesus to walk a few miles with you today, what would you want to talk about?
   - That I get really tired walking very far
   - A hard time I'm going through
   - My relationships
   - Nothing; just to walk quietly with him

- Finding meaning in my work
- Other _______________

6. During your walk with the resurrected Jesus, what might he bring up as an area of your life he'd like to start changing?

OUR STORY (all) 

7. What would be the best way to describe your current "walk" with Jesus?
   - Up and down
   - Growing
   - Pretty good
   - Slipping
   - Other _______________

8. Wherever you are, what step might you take this week to improve your "walk" with Jesus?

   ____

   ____

9. How do you want this group to support you, in the next week?

IN BETWEEN (individual)

- Have you started working yet on the step you described in #8?
- How do you need God's Spirit to help you? Can you ask him specifically?
- Keep notes of how God helps you.

58 JESUS APPEARS TO THOMAS (JOHN 20:24-31)

What is the BEST/WORST practical joke you've been part of?

"I'm known for my sponge cakes —made from real sponges!

I've pulled that prank on coworkers, students, relatives, friends ... everyone! I guess it's time to play it on my grandsons!"

BACK STORY*: The **Gospel** writers are transparent about the fact that the original **Disciples** at first could not believe that Jesus rose from the dead. Thomas heard from the others that Jesus was alive, but was not with them when Jesus first appeared to them behind locked doors. Feeling perhaps that he had once been mistaken about who Jesus was, he appears reluctant to buy into a resurrection story. Eight days later, Jesus appears again and invites Thomas to check him out. Jesus comments about those who will become believers some day without ever seeing him in person.

Read | Discuss Questions

²⁴One of the twelve disciples, Thomas (nicknamed the Twin), was not with the others when Jesus came. ²⁵They told him, "We have seen the Lord!"
But he replied, "I won't believe it unless I see the nail wounds in his hands, put my fingers into them, and place my hand into the wound in his side."
²⁶Eight days later the disciples were together again, and this time Thomas was with them. The doors were locked; but suddenly, as before, Jesus was standing among them. "Peace be with you," he said. ²⁷Then he said to Thomas, "Put your finger here, and look at my hands. Put your hand into the wound in my side. Don't be faithless any longer. Believe!"
²⁸"My Lord and my God!" Thomas exclaimed.
²⁹Then Jesus told him, "You believe because you have seen me. Blessed are those who believe without seeing me."
Purpose of the Book
³⁰The disciples saw Jesus do many other miraculous signs in addition to the ones recorded in this book. ³¹But these are written so that you may continue to believe that Jesus is the Messiah, the Son of God, and that by believing in him you will have life by the power of his name.

—John 20:24–31 (NLT)

*Parallel accounts: Mark 16:14;
Luke 24: 36–46

1. Thomas didn't have the benefit of hearing from the women who found the tomb empty, or of being present when Jesus first appeared to the disciples. Where do you think Thomas was? (Where would *you* have been?)
   - Sorting things out
   - Given up hope
   - Just in the wrong place, at the wrong time
   - Other _______________

2. What do you think Thomas meant when he said, "I won't believe it unless I see the nail wounds in his hands … and place my hand into the wound in his side"?
   - "This is too crazy to believe."
   - "I want hard proof."
   - "I want to believe, but …"
   - "I can't take having my heart crushed again."
   - Other _______________

3. Each time Jesus appears to his disciples, he starts with the statement, "Peace be with you." Why do you think he does that?
    - They're still terrified of the religious leaders.
    - He just showed up without opening the door!
    - He's wanting them to start trusting him.
    - It makes a good opening line.
    - Other _______________

4. Note Jesus' tone with Thomas. How would *you* have responded to him?
    - Tenderly, understanding his feeling of loss
    - Scolding him to just believe
    - Frustrated that he doesn't get the story yet
    - Other _______________

5. Who does Thomas remind you of?
    - A science teacher
    - Myself
    - A person with honest doubts
    - A friend of mine
    - Other _______________

6. When have you felt like Thomas must have felt or gone through what he went through?
    - When I lost someone really close to me, through death or broken relationship
    - When a friend betrayed me
    - When God didn't seem to answer my prayer
    - Other _______________

7. How have you worked through those feelings like Thomas?

    Or have you?

OUR STORY (all) 

8. When you struggle with trusting God, what do you find helpful?
    - Being honest with God and sharing my feelings
    - Reading the Bible
    - I'm still struggling and don't have answers yet
    - Talking with my pastor
    - Sharing with friends
    - Other

9. What one big idea from this story gives you the most encouragement for the coming week?

    ____

    ____

10. How do you need this group to pray with you?

IN BETWEEN (individual)

- Write down the "encouraging idea" from #9, and post it in a place where you can see it every day.

- Who will you try to encourage this week, as you're being encouraged?

59 JESUS REINSTATES PETER (JOHN 21:15-25)

 **GATHER** (all)

Choose one:

- What is your favorite food?

- Do you have a "forgiveness" story? Tell it briefly.

BACK STORY: In one of the last "appearance stories," **John** records a conversation between Jesus and Peter. Jesus asks Peter three times about his commitment to him. (Some see this as related to the three times Peter denied even knowing Jesus.) In the end, Peter is assured he is still one of the team and is given his assignment. Curious about John's future, he is told to focus on his own mission. John ends his **Gospel** by telling us there is a lot more he could have told us about Jesus.

 **FINDING MY STORY in GOD'S STORY** (groups of 3–5)

15After breakfast, Jesus said to Simon Peter, "Simon, son of John, do you love me more than these?"

"Yes, Master, you know I love you."

Jesus said, "Feed my lambs."

16He then asked a second time, "Simon, son of John, do you love me?"

"Yes, Master, you know I love you."

Jesus said, "Shepherd my sheep."

17-19Then he said it a third time: "Simon, son of John, do you love me?"

Peter was upset that he asked for the third time, "Do you love me?" so he answered, "Master, you know everything there is to know. You've got to know that I love you."

Jesus said, "Feed my sheep. I'm telling you the very truth now: When you were young you dressed yourself and went wherever you wished, but when you get old you'll have to stretch out your hands while someone else dresses you and takes you where you don't want to go." He said this to hint at the kind of death by which Peter would glorify God. And then he commanded, "Follow me."

20-21Turning his head, Peter noticed the disciple Jesus loved following right behind. When Peter noticed him, he asked Jesus, "Master, what's going to happen to him?"

22-23Jesus said, "If I want him to live until I come again, what's that to you? You— follow me." That is how the rumor got out among the brothers that this disciple wouldn't die. But that is not what Jesus said. He simply said, "If I want him to live until I come again, what's that to you?"

24This is the same disciple who was eye-witness to all these things and wrote them down. And we all know that his eyewitness account is reliable and accurate.

25There are so many other things Jesus did. If they were all written down, each of them, one by one, I can't imagine a world big enough to hold such a library of books.

—John 21:15–25 (MSG)

178

What is your FAVORITE food?

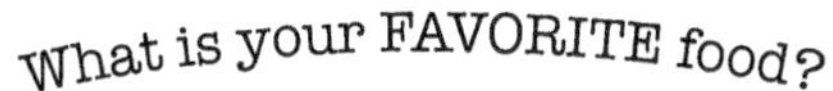

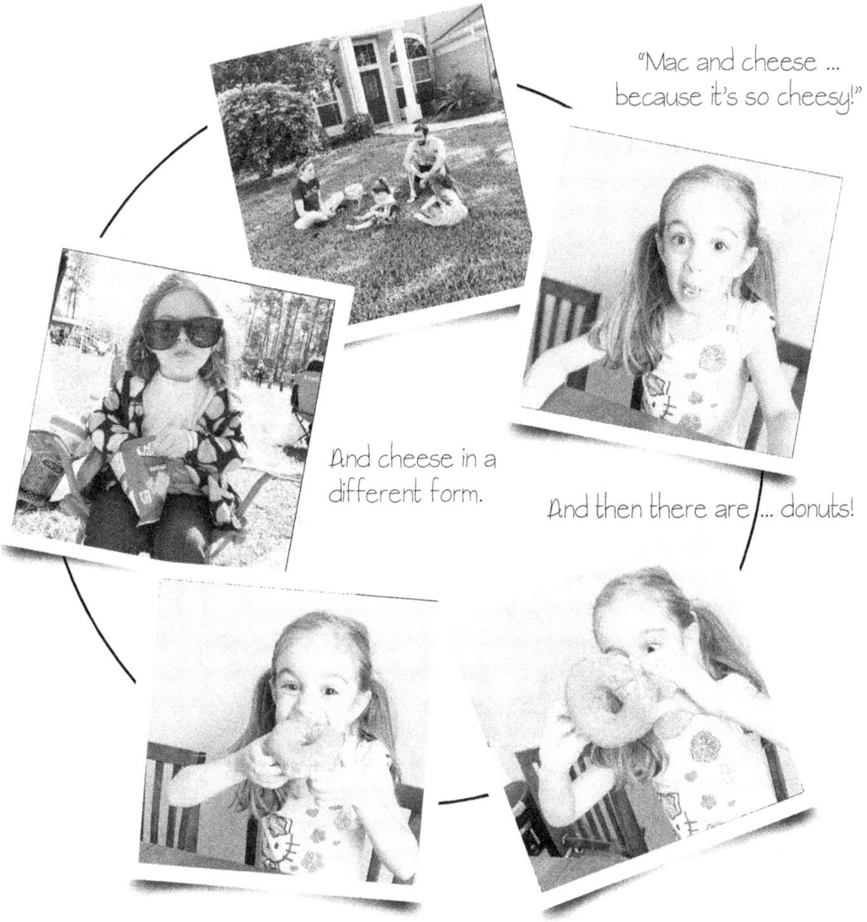

1. The earlier part of this story tells us that Peter and other disciples returned home from Jerusalem—and went fishing. If you'd been with them, why would you have been fishing when Jesus found you?
    - Taking a break
    - Returning to something familiar
    - Trying to put our lives back together
    - Obeying Jesus' instructions to go to Galilee and wait
    - Other ____________________

2. Why do you think Jesus cooked and shared breakfast with them?
    - To remind them, again, that he really was risen
    - To show, by eating with them, that he forgave them for failing him
    - To remind them of the significance of the Last Supper

3. After breakfast Jesus took Peter for a walk. What do you think was going through Peter's mind?
   - "Oh no! He's going to do this in front of my friends."
   - "I think I'm going to wet my robe."
   - "Finally! We can clear the air."
   - "Am I in for it now!"
   - Other _______________

4. Why do you think Jesus waited until this moment to confront Peter, instead of when he first appeared to his followers after the Resurrection?

5. Put yourself in Peter's sandals. Why do you think Jesus asked him, "Do you love me," three times?
   - To get his undivided attention
   - To enforce the point that he was forgiven
   - To match the times that Peter had denied knowing Jesus
   - Other _______________

6. If Jesus asked you to take a walk with him, what penetrating question might he ask you?
   - Same one: "Do you love me?"
   - "What are you doing with your life?"
   - I'm not sure.
   - "When will you let me be really important to you?"
   - Other _______________

7. How might you put Jesus' statement, "Take care of my sheep" into practice?
   - Love Jesus by being loving to others
   - Be less concerned about myself
   - Be more diligent in living Jesus' way
   - Other _______________

8. What helps you the most, when you've really messed up or hurt someone?
   - Talking with a friend
   - Don't have a good answer, yet
   - Talking with the people I've hurt
   - Prayer
   - Reading the Bible
   - Other _______________

OUR STORY (all) 

9. What part of this group meeting has been the most encouraging and helpful to you? Who or what made it encouraging?

10. How did you encourage someone this week. How did they respond?

11. What do you need prayer for?

IN BETWEEN (individual)

- Do some "internal inventory." Where have you hurt someone, maybe even unintentionally? How might you begin to help heal that relationship?

- What step will you try this week to help begin the healing?

60 JESUS' ASCENSION & GREAT COMMISSION

(ACTS 1:1-11 & MATTHEW 28:16-20)

GATHER (all)

Who would you pick to write a biography of your life?

What interesting thing do they know about you that the group should know?

BACK STORY*: Jesus finished his earthbound mission and is returning to God's side. These verses in Mathew, known as the Great Commission, record Jesus' words as he turns over authority to his followers to do what they've been trained to do—make more disciples. Specific tasks are spelled out that describe that mission. In Acts, Luke tells where their task was to happen and of power they would soon receive. The Greek word "doubted" (as in Matthew 28:17) indicates not unbelief, but hesitancy in the face of a seemingly impossible task.

[1]In my former book, Theophilus, I wrote about all that Jesus began to do and to teach [2]until the day he was taken up to heaven, after giving instructions through the Holy Spirit to the apostles he had chosen. [3]After his suffering, he presented himself to them and gave many convincing proofs that he was alive. He appeared to them over a period of forty days and spoke about the kingdom of God. [4]On one occasion, while he was eating with them, he gave them this command: "Do not leave Jerusalem, but wait for the gift my Father promised, which you have heard me speak about. [5]For John baptized with water, but in a few days you will be baptized with the Holy Spirit."
[6]Then they gathered around him and asked him, "Lord, are you at this time going to restore the kingdom to Israel?"
[7]He said to them: "It is not for you to know the times or dates the Father has set by his own authority. [8]But you will receive power when the Holy Spirit comes on you; and you will be my witnesses in Jerusalem, and in all Judea and Samaria, and to the ends of the earth."
[9]After he said this, he was taken up before their very eyes, and a cloud hid him from their sight. [10]They were looking intently up into the sky as he was going, when suddenly two men dressed in white stood beside them. [11]"Men of Galilee," they said, "why do you stand here looking into the sky? This same Jesus, who has been taken from you into heaven, will come back in the same way you have seen him go into heaven."
—Acts 1:1–11 (NIV)

MORE OF THE STORY...
[16]Then the eleven disciples went to Galilee, to the mountain where Jesus had told them to go. [17]When they saw him, they worshiped him; but some doubted. [18]Then Jesus came to them and said, "All authority in heaven and on earth has been given to me. [19]Therefore go and make disciples of all nations, baptizing them in the name of the Father and of the Son and of the Holy Spirit, [20]and teaching them to obey everything I have commanded you. And surely I am with you always, to the very end of the age."
—Matthew 28:16–20

*Parallel account: Mark 16:15

1. Imagine standing on the hillside with Jesus and his followers. He gives a few final words and is gone. How would your response compare to or be different from that of the other disciples?

2. How would you describe Jesus' ascension to heaven in one word?
   - Sad—the end of his earthly ministry
   - Beginning—the start of a new phase of his ministry
   - Amazing—that would have been something to see!
   - Puzzling—did it really happen?
   - Other _______________

3. Review Acts 1:1–5. What do you think Luke wants Theophilus to understand the most?
   - God's Holy Spirit would be coming.
   - Jesus proved his resurrection in many places.
   - Jesus didn't just "fly off" after the resurrection.
   - Other _______________

4. The angels showed up after Jesus left. Write their message to the disciples in your own words; then read it to the group.

5. In Matthew's addition to the Ascension story, we get what is often called "the Great Commission." What is the good news you see in Matthew 28:18–20?
   * I have a mission to share Jesus' life and love.
   * I'm not alone on the mission.
   * Baptism is an important symbol to "mark" Jesus' followers.
   * The Father, Jesus, and the Holy Spirit are all in on this together.
   * Other ___________________

6. As you review this story of Jesus' Ascension and the mission he calls each person to, what is the most overwhelming for you?

   What inspires you the most?

OUR STORY (all) 

7. As a group, discuss some ways that you each might use your gifts to live out the "Great Commission" in your neighborhood. How might you better serve, encourage, bless, and share Jesus' love?

   How might you as a combined group live out the "Great Commission?"

   Write down several ideas that resonate with you.

8. How can this group encourage you and pray for you?

IN BETWEEN

* Using the notes you took in #7, what will you begin doing this week to live out the "Great Commission" where you live, work, and play?
* How do you need God's Spirit to help you live out the mission God has for you?

~ THE END NOTES ~

CHECK THIS OUT!

The next few pages contain **background** about the stories you've been discussing—the four Gospels in the New Testament: Matthew, Mark, Luke and John.

And, as promised, you can find additional information about **bolded words** in the BACK STORY (among others) in these END NOTES and in the KEY WORDS INDEX beginning on page 186.

 # END NOTES

Gospel/The Gospels

The word Gospel means Good News—the Good News of Jesus' birth, death, and resurrection and the fulfillment of God's Salvation promised in the Old Testament. Many "gospels" existed by the end of the first century A.D. (C.E.) as attested to by Luke (1:1). Only the Gospels (capital G) of Matthew, Mark, Luke, and John were regarded from earliest Christian history as canonical—meeting the standards required to be accepted as authoritative and true accounts of God's actions. The authors did not claim to present exhaustive accounts of Jesus' life (John 20:30, Luke 1:1–4). Each contained enough to accomplish the purpose of its author. (See Matt. 1:1, Mark 1:1, Luke 1:1–2, John 20:31.) Each author arranged his material for his own specific instructional purposes. The differences represent different purposes. The similarities reflect a common background and central truth about Jesus' life and ministry. None claim to be chronological accounts. Each was written sometime after Christ's resurrection (15–30 years) and reflect oral and written material from the Apostles' teachings following Pentecost (See Acts 2:42). Each book focuses a disproportionate amount of its space on the events during Jesus' last weeks, and on his death and resurrection.

The Gospel of Matthew

The author was also known as Levi (Mark 2:14; Luke 5:27). Matthew was one of the 12 original disciples. He was Jewish, and a tax collector for the Roman authorities, when Jesus called him. As a tax collector, he was a record keeper and thus, some believe, wrote from the records he kept during his years of following Jesus. He wrote his account primarily for a Jewish audience to show them that Jesus of Nazareth was the long-awaited, promised Messiah. He traces Jesus' heritage back to Abraham. He quotes Old Testament passages more than any other Gospel writer. Matthew constructed his narrative around five distinct conversations: The Sermon on the Mount (5–7), Instruction to Disciples (10), Kingdom Parables (13,) Nature of True Discipleship (18), and End Times (24–25). Little else is known of Matthew. As we look at the picture of Jesus in Matthew, we see the anointed one, a king in the line of David.

The Gospel of Mark

The author's given name was John Mark. His mother was Mary, who owned the house where the disciples gathered for prayer (Acts 12:12). Mark was Jewish and a companion of Paul (2 Timothy 4:11) and Peter (1 Peter 5:13). He was a cousin of Barnabas (Colossians 4:10) and began the first missionary journey with Barnabas and Paul (Saul, Acts 12:25). He was a missionary to Cyprus with Barnabas (Acts 15:38–39). Early church leaders referred to him as "the interpreter for Peter" and believed his book represented the teachings of Peter. His Gospel is a fast-paced narrative. It contains details only an eye witness would have known (4:37; 10:16; 10:21; 9:36; 15:21). As we look at the picture of Jesus in Mark, we see his servanthood.

The Gospel of Luke

Luke was not Jewish, but Greek. He was a companion of the Apostle Paul, and a physician (Colossians 4:14). He researched other accounts that had been in circulation and interviewed surviving witnesses and disciples to write both the Gospel of Luke (Luke 1:1) and the Book of Acts—the first thoroughly researched history of the early Christian Church (Acts 1:1). He regularly tied events in his writing to known historical personages (Luke 3:1–2) so that they could be dated. The Gospel of Luke was written some 30 years after the resurrection of Jesus and used the best Greek language in the New Testament. He spoke more of women (43 times) than Matthew and Mark (a combined 49 times). In Luke's Gospel, Jesus is often seen in the company of the poor and marginalized people in society. As we look at the picture of Jesus in Luke, we see his humanity.

The Gospel of John

John was Jewish. Along with his brother James, he was among the first four chosen by Jesus (Mark 1:19–20). He was the last surviving and believed to be the only original disciple not martyred for his faith. He also wrote First, Second, and Third John, and Revelation. He wrote as an "eye witness" (John 1:14; 21:24, 1 John 1:3). At the end of his life, he was in exile on the Island of Patmos, off the coast of present-day Turkey (Revelation 1:9). John began Jesus' history with God, long before creation (John 1:1–5). His only narrative of Jesus' birth was given in John 1:14. His choice and organization of stories was clearly stated by his purpose statement (John 20:30–31). He supported his claim to who Jesus was with seven "I Am" statements by Jesus and paraded 27 witnesses (interviews) before us to attest to Jesus' divinity and his humanity. As we look at the picture of Jesus in John, we see his divinity.

 # KEY WORDS

Augustus Caesar

The grand-nephew and adopted son of Julius Caesar, Octavius was emperor. The name Augustus was given to him by the Roman Senate. He ruled for 40 years, beginning around 27 B.C. Our calendar month of August is named for him.

Bethlehem

The place of Jesus' birth. It was King David's ancestral home, located less than seven miles south of Jerusalem. Historical records validate the Roman practice of requiring the heads of households to return to their family's ancestral city to be counted during a census.

Capernaum

A city located off the northeast side of the Sea of Galilee. Jesus moved there from Nazareth at the beginning of his ministry (Matthew 4:12–13). Several of Jesus' miracles were done here (Mark 2:1–12; Luke 4:23; John 4:46–54). Peter lived here at the time (Matthew 8:5, 14). Luke tells us Andrew, James, and John were all partners with Peter in fishing here (Luke 5:10).

Chief Priest(s)

The term Chief Priests referred to the larger group of former high priests and other priests responsible for the daily oversite and operation of Temple worship. Some of these served on the Sanhedrin.

Christ

A title given to Jesus, not his last name. "Christ" is the Greek word *Christos*, meaning "anointed one" or "chosen one." The Hebrew word is *Mashiach*, or

"Messiah." Thus, "Jesus Christ" means "Jesus the Messiah" or "Jesus the Anointed One."

Demons
In the Bible, demons were understood to be fallen angels under the direction of Satan.

Denarius/denarii
A small Roman silver coin, equivalent to one day's wages.

Disciple
An apprentice of a rabbi. A gifted Jewish boy, usually in his mid-teens, could approach a Jewish rabbi and ask if he could "follow" him—become his disciple. The rabbi—if he felt the student was able to replicate that rabbi's interpretation on the oral and written Law, and had the potential to become like the rabbi—would choose the young man and begin his training. Those not "chosen" would end their formal schooling and begin to learn a trade. John the Baptist had disciples (John 1:35), as did many Pharisees in Jesus' day.

Elizabeth
An older relative (cousin) of Mary. Her husband was Zachariah, a priest. She was six months' pregnant when Jesus' mother, Mary, first visited her. She was the mother of John the Baptist. (Luke 1:5, 8–10.)

Elisha
A prophet in Israel, the northern ten tribes. (2 Kings 2:1–2.)

Engaged
Engaged Jewish couples were legally referred to as "husband and wife," and their relationship could be broken only by divorce. It is unclear whether Jewish law required chastity in all cases before the wedding. The bride usually lived with her parents until the actual marriage ceremony, at which time she would be brought to the home that the groom had prepared. The marriage would also include a celebration feast.

Feasts
The are many feasts listed in the Pentateuch (the first five books of the Old Testament). When possible, devout Jews from all over the world would travel to Jerusalem to celebrate three of these: The Feast of Passover, the Feast of Pentecost, and the Feast of Tabernacles.

Feast of Passover
Celebrating Yahweh's deliverance from slavery in Egypt when an Angel of Death "passed over" all who had posted blood on their doorposts (Exodus 12:11–30). The firstborn of men and beasts in Egypt died that night. It was one of the three Pilgrimage Feasts.

Feast of Pentecost (Shavuot)
Also known as the Feast of Weeks. This celebration happened at harvest time, 50 days (7 weeks) after the Passover/ Feast of First Fruits (Leviticus 23:15–16). It was during this celebration that the Holy Spirit was given to the disciples gathered in an upper room, 10 days after the Ascension of Jesus (Acts 2: 1–4). It was one of the three Pilgrimage Feasts where Jews from all over traveled to Jerusalem. Because this happened later in the spring, it usually drew the larger crowds.

Feast of Tabernacles (Succoth)
Also known as the Feast of Booths, an annual celebration of God's caring for the Israelites for 40 years in the wilder-

ness. Families would build small sheds or booths to live in during this festival (Deuteronomy 16:13–17). It was one of the three Pilgrimage Feasts.

Gabriel
One of only two angels named in Protestant versions of the Bible. (Michael is the other.) See Daniel 9:21, 10:13; Jude 9. A third, Lucifer (Satan)—from the Latin translation of the Hebrew text for "day star" or "bright one"—is referred to in Isaiah 14:12. The name "Lucifer" is found only in the King James and New King James versions of the Bible.

Galilee
A province in northwest Palestine, north of Jerusalem. The Sea of Galilee and the villages of Nazareth, Capernaum, and Cana, all mentioned in the accounts of Jesus' life and ministry, were located in Galilee. Jesus lived in the region for some 30 years and much of his ministry occurred there. Many of Jesus' miracles happened here.

Gentile(s)
The word itself means "nations" and comes from a Latin translation of the Hebrew word. It is a term used in the New Testament of the Bible for any non-Jewish people or nation. In the Old Testament, the Hebrew word is simply translated "nation."

Herod
The appointed Roman king of Israel from 37–4 B.C., also known as Herod the Great. He was king during Jesus' birth (Matt. 2:1–19; Luke 1:5). His sons ruled different provinces of Palestine during Jesus' life and ministry. Known for his insecurities, he had his wife and several of his sons killed. He was responsible for the killing of all infants in Bethlehem in an effort to kill Jesus (Matthew 2:1–8). To win favor with the Jews, he was responsible for the remodeling and expanding of the Temple. Several of his sons were also known as King Herod (Herod Antipas, Herod Philip, Herod Agrippa I, Herod Agrippa II) and are mentioned in the New Testament.

High Priest
Sometimes referred to as chief priest (singular), the High Priest was the chief/head among the other priests. He was head of the Sanhedrin and the chief religious leader in Israel. Originally high priests had to come from the hereditary bloodline of Aaron, Moses' brother, and members of the tribe of Levi (Exodus 28:1). By Jesus' day, the high priest was more of a political appointee of the Roman government. The high priest was the only person allowed to enter the Holy of Holies (the inner sanctuary of the Temple) on the annual Day of Atonement, where he offered a sacrifice for the sins of the nation.

Isaiah
A prophet in Judah, the southern tribes in ancient Israel. His name in Hebrew means "God is Salvation." Isaiah's prophecies are recorded in the Old Testament book that bears his name. He was a prophet from 740–700 B.C. Some of the best-known passages of the Bible and classical music are found in this book (Isaiah 9, 11, 40).

Jerusalem
Established as the capital city of the combined kingdom of Israel under King David. The location of the Temple.

Jesus
A name from the Hebrew name *Yeshua*, meaning "to deliver," or "to rescue."

Jesus would not have had a last name other than perhaps "son of Joseph."

John the Baptist
The miracle son of the Priest Zachariah and Elizabeth (Luke 1: 5ff) in their old age. He was believed to be a cousin to Jesus based on the relationship of Elizabeth to Mary. This forerunner of Jesus lived in the desert country (Mark 1: 4, 6) and preached the coming of the Kingdom of God. He was the first witness to who Jesus was in John's Gospel (John 1:29) and baptized Jesus (Matthew 3:13) at the inauguration of Jesus' ministry. Several of John's disciples became Jesus' disciples. He was imprisoned and later murdered on orders of Herod the Tetrarch (Matthew 14: 3–12).

King David
The second and most honored king of Israel (1 Samuel 16:1ff). As a boy, he was a shepherd of his father's flocks in Bethlehem. The greatest number of Psalms in the Old Testament book of Psalms are attributed to David. The promised Messiah was prophesied to come from the lineage (as a descendant) of King David.

Kingdom of Heaven/Kingdom of God
These terms are used interchangeably in the New Testament and refer to the rule or reign of God over creation, nations, and people. "Kingdom of Heaven" is found only in Matthew. "Kingdom of God" is found in all four Gospels— some 80 times. The coming of the Kingdom of God was a major focus of Jesus' preaching (Matthew 4:23). See also the Kingdom of Light and Kingdom of the Lord. Jesus describes the Kingdom in parables (Matthew 13:31–32; Mark 4:26–29, 30–32; Luke 13:18–19, 20–21).

Laws of Moses
This term refers to the first five books of the Old Testament—the Pentateuch. Moses is credited with assembling and recording these books. These books contain myriad, explicit and comprehensive instructions for all aspects of Jewish life. Luke notes three Mosaic requirements for Jewish parents: circumcision, the ritual purification of the mother, and the dedication of the firstborn. See Genesis 17:12; Exodus 13:12; and Leviticus 12:6–8.

Legion
A term often used symbolically in the Bible to simply mean many. A legion was a Roman military unit of 6,000 soldiers plus 120 calvary.

Leprosy
An infectious disease that causes disfiguring skin sores and nerve damage. See Leviticus 13:45 for how this disease was handled in New Testament times. See also, Leviticus 14:1–57 and how to be declared "clean" by a priest.

Lord
The Greek word *kurios* is translated "master" or "lord." In the New Testament, it is the Greek word used when translating the Hebrew name for God— *Yahweh* or *Jehovah* (Acts 2:36). Roman coinage bore the inscription "Caesar is Lord."

Mary Magdalene
A follower of Jesus who was present at the crucifixion (John19:25) and burial of Jesus when others left. She was one of the first to discover the empty tomb (John 20:1), the first to whom Jesus appeared after his resurrection, and the first to announce the Good News of Jesus' resurrection (John 20:11). "Mag-

dalene" indicates her hometown—Mary of Magdala—on the shores of the Sea of Galilee. Mary Magdalene is one of many Mary's named in the Gospels, and little light is shed on her background. She has been called saint and sinner in writings from the second century on. Luke appears to identify her as one cured of seven demons (ailments), well to do, one of many women who provided for the disciples out of their resources (Luke 8:1–3).

Miracle
A word used to identify extraordinary acts of Jesus and later those of the disciples. Three Greek words are translated as "miracle" as well as "power," "signs," and "wonders." Miracles were used to point to Jesus' person and power and as signs of the coming of the Kingdom of God. Miracles were not "sideshow" acts to attract large crowds. Jesus often told individuals to say nothing about a healing miracle (Matthew 8:3–4; 9:29–30).

Naaman
A Syrian military leader who was cured of leprosy (2 Kings 5:1–15).

Nazareth
The boyhood home of Jesus after his parents returned from exile in Egypt (Matthew 2:21–23). It was located in the province of Galilee in northern Israel. The insignificance of this town in Jesus' day can be found in Nathanael's mocking reference recorded in John 1:46.

Passover
Celebrating Yahweh's deliverance from slavery in Egypt when an Angel of Death "passed over" all who had posted blood on their doorposts (Exodus 12:11–30). The firstborn of men and beasts in Egypt died that night. It was one of the three Pilgrimage Feasts.

Pharisee(s)
One of four groups in Jewish society in Jesus' time. Their name can be rendered, Separatist. They were the "legalists" of the day, very active politically, and took much too much pride in keeping the Ten Commandments and hundreds more regulations they adopted to keep them from breaking the Ten. They held to both the written law (Old Testament) and the oral traditions. Unlike other Jewish groups, namely the Sadducees, they believed in a resurrection.

Pontius Pilate
A Roman governor (prefect), appointed by Emperor Tiberius, over Judaea, Samaria, and Idumaea. He served from 26–36 A.D. (C.E.). A Roman governor had command of the soldiers in his provinces, was charged with maintaining order in his provinces, was a judge, and had the sole power to order executions.

Priest
There were 24 divisions (groups) of priests that took turns administering the sacred duties at the Temple in Jesus' day (Luke 1:5, 8–10). A priest spoke for God, administered the daily sacrifices, and performed other sacred duties.

Quirinius
Historical documents place a Publius Sulpicius Quirinius in Syria around 6 B.C.

Ruler of the Jews
Jewish "rulers" were the 70 members of the Sanhedrin. They are also called the "Council of the Elders," or simply "elders" in the Gospels and Acts (Matthew 27:1–2; Acts 22:5, NASB).

Rabbi

A scholar of Jewish law and a teacher. Rabbis were Jewish males, at least 30 years of age, who had successfully passed through years of study and had been discipled by another rabbi. Training in the Jewish scriptures, oral traditions, and interpretations began at the age of five for Jewish boys. By the age of ten, most Jewish boys would have memorized the Pentateuch—the first five books of the Old Testament (Luke 2:39–40). Those who aspired to become rabbis continued this training beyond the age of 15, others went on to learn a trade. A rabbi's means of teaching often consisted largely of asking questions and answering questions with questions. We see Rabbi Jesus using this method (Matthew 22:17–20; Matthew 12:9–12).

Sanhedrin

The Romans granted limited jurisdiction to this body to act as the civil and religious authority (John 18:31). The Sanhedrin had 70 members, plus the High Priest as the chief officer. Members are also called the "Council of the Elders, Jewish "rulers," or simply "elders" in the Gospels and Acts (Matthew 27:1–2; Acts 22:5 NASB).

Sabbath

This Jewish day of worship was observed from sundown on Friday until sundown on Saturday. The Hebrews (Jews) worshiped on the seventh day of the week, the day God rested after creation (Genesis 2:1–3). The Jewish day followed the pattern found in the creation story, with each new day starting in the evening. "And there was evening and there was morning, the first day" (Genesis 1:1–3).

Samaria/Samaritans

In the Old Testament, Samaria was the capital city of the northern ten tribes of Israel after the kingdom split. In Jesus' day, the term referred to a region. Conquered by Assyria (2 Kings 17:6), Samaria's citizens were resettled to other parts of the Empire, and the region was resettled by captives (2 Kings 17:24) from other nations. Because of the mixed racial bloodlines that resulted, Samaritans were no longer considered Jews (Ezra 4:1–3). Samaritans worshipped at Mount Gerizim instead of the Temple in Jerusalem.

Savior

A common word in the ancient world. Victorious military leaders were seen as saviors. Jesus' name means to save, to rescue, or "God is salvation" (Matthew 1:21).

Sea of Galilee

A large body of water called by several different names in the Old and New Testaments, including Lake of Gennesaret (Luke 5:1), and the Sea of Tiberias (John 21:1). The Jordan River runs through it. The topography of the area around the Sea made it susceptible to sudden storms when cool winds blew over the warmer sea waters from the mountains on the east.

Sermon on the Mount

Chapters 5–7 of Matthew's Gospel are a collection of Jesus' teaching on the Kingdom of Heaven. This segment starts with what is called the Beatitudes and moves on to teachings on marriage, prayer, fasting, judgment, and others. Luke's Gospel has a similar collection of teachings sometimes called the Sermon on the Plains (Luke 6:17–49).

Sinners

A term used for individuals whose lifestyle and actions were such that they were considered outside God's grace and thus were to be avoided (Psalm 1:1; Isaiah 59:2).

Son of God

Many early Roman rulers were referred to as "son of God" or "son of a deity." Matthew uses this title for Jesus to identify him as the Old Testament's promised Messiah.

Snake

For the story of Moses and the healing power of a brass serpent referred to by Jesus, see Numbers 21:6–9.

Synagogues

The center of Jewish life, education, and worship after the destruction of the Temple and Israel's captivity in Babylon. Jesus was regularly found in a synagogue on the sabbath (Luke 4:16).

Tax Collectors

Rome hired local citizens in captive countries to collect fees and taxes from their fellow citizens. The King James Version Bible uses the term "publicans" in place of tax collectors. They were known to charge more than the required amount and to keep the excess (Luke 19:1–10).

Teachers of the Law

This title is also referred to as Scribes in other translations.

Temple

The center of worship for Jews since the days of Solomon. Prior to the Temple being built, Jewish worship took place in the Tabernacle—a large tent structure that could be taken down and would travel with the tribes. The original Temple—built by Solomon, David's son—was destroyed by the Babylonians. The second, a poor copy, was built by the Jews who returned from Babylonian captivity. Herod the Great remodeled and expanded this second Temple—the one mentioned in the Gospels and Acts. It was destroyed by Rome in 70 A.D. The were several sections to the Temple area itself, all on different levels—the Holy of Holies, the Court of the Priest, The Court of Israel (men only), the Court of the Women, and the Court of the Gentiles.

Unclean

Leviticus and Deuteronomy contain many "laws" about things God told Moses were "clean" and "unclean" before the age of modern medicine. These laws were designed to protect the health and welfare of the people. Mark 5:24–34 refers back to Leviticus 15:19ff. A menstruating woman, anyone touching or being touched by her, or anyone coming in contact with human blood was considered "unclean."

Wineskins

These were cleaned animal hides used to carry or store new wine. As the new wine continued to ferment, the skins would expand and stretch. If new wine were placed in a stretched, used skin, it would likely burst the skin.

Zachariah

The husband of Mary's older cousin, Elizabeth. Zechariah was a priest of the division of Abijah. (See **Priest**.)

Biblical and Theological Sources consulted:

- *A Critical Lexicon and Concordance to the English and Greek New Testament*
- *Baker Encyclopedia of the Bible*
- *Beacon Bible Commentary of the New Testament*
- *Lexham Bible Dictionary*
- *Manners & Customs of the Bible*
- *The Bible Exposition Commentary*
- *The New Bible Commentary*
- *Smithsonian Magazine*
- *Zondervan Pictorial Encyclopedia of the Bible*

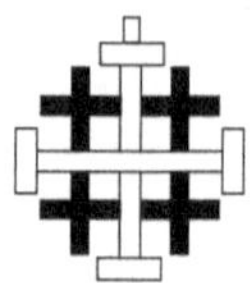# LEADER'S GUIDE FOR CELL GROUPS

FIRST THINGS FIRST

Beyond the notes at the beginning of this book, here are additional, detailed guidelines that may be helpful.

- These notes are primarily for Cell Group leaders. However, whether an administrative board, a sports-bar Bible study or something in between, every group should become a community of people who live in love with one another and on mission to those outside the group. So, the following guidelines are adaptable to most any setting.

- While "Cell Group" is a generic term for a small community of people, we often use the more specific term Village Group because it has richer, community meaning.

    A Village is a place where:
    o Everyone belongs,
    o People feel safe to tell their story,
    o Everyone is being equipped for ministry and service,
    o Everyone is cared for,
    o There is a common mission, and

    o You can always come home.

    Consider using the term to help your group catch the deeper meaning of why they are together.

- RECRUIT AN APPREN-TICE-LEADER to become a future group leader. This will be vital when beginning to birth a new group.

    The Apprentice will work with you to grow to the point of group leadership. You will regularly meet with your Apprentice for coaching. You will want to give them experience guiding the group when you are present. Then, after a session they lead, of course, you can debrief the meeting. Never evaluate in front of the group.

SUBDIVIDE THE GROUP

When a group grows larger than SEVEN people, you should subdivide the group for at least part of your Cell Group session. You may notice that in a group larger than seven, about half of the group members join in discussion while the other half observe.

- The **ENTIRE GROUP** should meet together for the GATHERING question(s), a drink, and some finger food. People need a cup or mug to hold for ease of discussion.

- **THREE–FIVESOMES** are the best grouping for the FINDING MY STORY IN GOD'S STORY Bible study and discussion.

- **ALL group members** should re-join together for OUR STORY time. Group members can bring concerns they've shared in the three-fivesomes to this time.

- **EIGHTSOMES** or more are great for worship or singing, if you add those elements to the group time.

- While it's important to always plan to birth a new group, subdividing allows a group to grow to almost any size. This is particularly important if a group grows quickly, before an Apprentice-leader is ready to take leadership of the group.

THE QUESTIONS

The Session Agendas are created to take approximately 1.5 hours. Groups should not regularly go longer than that. Sometimes you may go shorter.

The questions are strategically worded and placed where they are to help the three stories connect around the Bible passage.

As the leader of the group, you should know your group. And since you know the purpose of the various questions (BELOW) feel free to rewrite or adapt the questions for your needs.

In addition, if discussion goes long on particular questions, don't panic, just cut somewhere else. HOWEVER, as you adapt, make sure to pick and choose from each type of question, keeping them in the correct sequence.

- **GATHERING**
  (approx. 15 min.)

  The **GATHERING** question(s) is to get the group thinking about the biblical topic in a non-threatening way; often producing laughter, bringing out positive endorphins and reducing barriers to the deeper questions that are coming.

  You may want to "toss" this question into conversation around a coffee pot in the kitchen, before sending the THREE-FIVESOMES off to various locations to study the Bible passage.

- **FINDING MY STORY IN GOD'S STORY (approx. 45 min.)**

The first 2 or 3 questions right after the Bible reading help people put themselves into the scripture passage.

The next few questions are to help the group **dig out some of the content**. You may want to add extra questions here. But **do it carefully** so you don't bog the group down or lose sight of the overall purpose. The temptation is to "go deeper" in study, which usually means learning facts instead of building healthy relationships around the Bible section.

- **OUR STORY (approx. 30 min.)**

This is the time when the group regathers to check in with one another. There are questions to answer or assignments to complete. Group members should report in from their previous missions, as well.

Use this time to pray for and encourage one another.

- **IN BETWEEN**

Remind the group members to pay attention to the IN BE-TWEEN notes, and to live on mission during the week—wherever they live, work, and play.

Once a month or so, you will want to find a way to serve together as a group, in your community, your city, or the world. Particularly look for opportunities to partner with agencies or groups who are making a positive difference in your area—whether faith-based or not.

In addition, every group should have an "empty chair." Then each group member remains constantly alert for friends and neighbors to fill the empty chair—to join your Cell Group.

It is important to plant the idea of MISSION or SERVICE at the very first gathering of the group; reinforcing it each time the group meets.

ABOUT PRAYING...

As part of each session, you may guide the group in various patterns of prayer so they can join in carrying one another's needs.

However, If you want your group members to be **scared spitless**, just ask one of them to pray out loud. If you want to teach them to actually pray for one another, suggest various forms of prayer, in a progressive pattern.

Here are some Levels of Prayer to introduce prayer to the group that will help each person begin praying aloud. You will decide when your group members are ready to move from one level to the next; think several weeks, not one week to the next.

Feel free to make adjustments as you sense they are needed.

Level 1: After the group has shared concerns, you pray out loud. As you model praying for the group, forget the special words or phrases you might have heard. That's what scares people out of feeling competent to pray. Just be yourself conversationally with God.

Level 2: After requests have been shared, ask for an equal number of volunteers to pray for those requests—each one praying a brief prayer for one request.

Level 3: Invite **two** or **three** group members to pray, then you conclude. This takes courage for those who've never prayed out loud before because you've not assigned them a topic to pray about.

Don't be afraid of silence for a moment or two. If no one prays after a lengthy time of silence, go ahead and pray out loud.

Level 4: Ask the group to sit or stand in a circle and pray out loud around the circle by saying something like, "Dear God,

this is ________ . Thank you for ________. Amen."

If anyone is too uncomfortable with this plan, they can pray silently when their turn comes. They will simply say "Amen" to let the next person know when they have completed their silent prayer.

You may also try variations of any of these levels of prayer, such as having the group pray silently around the circle for the person on their left.

Before long you'll have the whole group easily praying for one another. They just have to discover that it's safe to say what they're really thinking and feeling without the pressure to produce some form of "magic" words for God.

Some CAUTIONS:
- NEVER let people "confess another person's sins." People are only allowed to talk about their own issues. You might need to interrupt an overly transparent person. This often happens between couples.

- Gossip can kill a group. Watch for prayer requests/concerns that are actually cloaked gossip.

- Sometimes one person may dominate conversation with their struggles for several meetings. As a leader, you may need to talk directly to such a person, in private. A group cannot do therapy for an individual. That takes special care from a professional.

READING THE BIBLE

It's not unusual for people to be called on to read in a group. However, it can strike terror in any introvert or person with reading difficulties. Use these guidelines when preparing to read the Bible passages together as a group—even if you've subdivided into THREE-FIVE-SOMES for the Bible study time.

- Unless you know a person really well, and their reading ability, never surprise a person by calling on them to read. This is especially true when reading the Bible, which may have difficult-to-pronounce words or complicated language structures.

- The best way to prepare a person to read is to ask them before the session starts. Give them the opportunity to review the passage and plan for any difficult words or phrases.

- If a person volunteers to read but then has difficulty getting through a passage, feel free to assist them by giving them a word or two and letting them attempt to continue.

- Thank and compliment readers, particularly when the passage or pronunciations have been difficult.

BIRTHING NEW GROUPS—NEVER SPLIT

You may not plan to birth a new group during the first few months of your Cell Group's life. However, if you continue meeting longer than about 12 months, you'll want to start the birthing process.

Here are a few important tips for introducing the birthing idea to the group members, and actually beginning to birth a new Cell Group.

1. **Always us the term *birthing*.** We **never split** groups. Birthing is the healthy beginning of another group out of an original Cell Group.

2. Once a group reaches 10 to 12 people, the group needs to start planning the birth. However, "birthing" should be discussed at the very first group meeting, and every meeting thereafter, so no one is surprised.

   Remember that you can effectively use **subdividing** until you're ready for the birth.

3. Every group must have an **Apprentice** as well as a Leader.

When birthing a new group, the **original Leader**, with **three to six** people from the original group, are commissioned to leave the original Cell Group to start the new one.

The **Apprentice** stays as leader of the original group. Both groups must then quickly find new Apprentice leaders.

4. The best way to birth a new group is for the current Leader to collect an affinity group from the original group (for example, parents of 2- year-olds). Those three to six people will invite others to join them. They might even start the new group studying something about parenting toddlers. After about one series of "affinity studies" they will move back to their regular Cell Group Relational Bible study.

5. Birthing is enhanced when the original group and the newly-birthed group create a celebration party for the launch. You also might consider periodic family-reunion parties for a couple of months.

6. Everyone is responsible for recruiting new group members to fill the vacancies created by the birth—and to grow the newly birthed group. Never forget the **empty chair**.

LAST BUT NOT LEAST

To be most effective in your ministry as a Group Leader, you need to start seeing yourself as a **SHEPHERD** to your Village Group. That's right, a SHEPHERD, even if that is not your strongest gift area.

Before you reject the idea outright, think about it for a minute. Your faith community probably has other people whom you call Shepherd or Pastor. She or he oversees the larger ministry of the congregation. However, you probably noticed that there is no way for one person to meet a congregation's many needs. The best care comes when a cell group, led by its Leader, takes responsibility for its team members. You are the front-line shepherd to your "congregation."

This also gives you the opportunity to recruit those in your group who have the Shepherd gifting/passion, and coach them to begin caring for the other group members.

In other words, you are modeling the life of a disciple. **And disciples disciple others to follow Jesus!**

This Shepherding model may mean leading the Cell Group sessions. But it will also include staying alert to the individual emotional, physical, and spiritual needs of your group members. It could also mean hospital visitation or rallying the group for special support of a group member who is facing a crisis.

Here's another way to think of it.

You are a **COACH**!

When you read that word Coach, your mind may think of coaches you've seen pace the sidelines of a court or field; some yelling, screaming and throwing things—others calmly watching and guiding the team.

Hundreds of years ago, before the word coach became a person, it described a vehicle. And that vehicle carried royalty—PRECIOUS CARGO.

Let that idea soak in your brain for a minute.

When you are Shepherding and Coaching your Cell Group, you are carrying precious cargo. You are helping God's Spirit (the Holy Spirit) move people from where they are right now to where God wants them to be, down the road.

But don't let that overwhelm you.

This is God's ministry, and you have the privilege of partnering with the Holy Spirit, who has been at work long before you got to this place. And you're coaching a group of people who can learn to care for one another.

So have fun watching what you and God can do together to grow your Cell Group into an amazing, healthy COMMUNITY!

Coaching for creating vibrant small group ministries is available. Contact Daryl L. Smith (Village Group Trainer | 5Q Coach/Trainer) at DarylSmith432@gmail.com or www.5QCentral.com.

Additional resources:
- *The End of Small Groups: Leading Incarnational Villages*; Amazon.com
- *Discovering Your Missional Potential: An Encounter With Ephesians 4 and How Jesus Lives It*; Amazom.com or https://5QCentral.com/product-category/books
- *Radical Journey: A Discipling Immersion with Jesus in the Sermon on the Mount*; Lulu.com.